THE ENLIGHTENED EGO

Discover
Your Ego's Purpose
and the
Path of Transcendence

KELLY BENINGA

Park Point
PRESS

Park Point Press | 573 Park Point Drive | Golden CO 80401

Contents

Acknowledgments

This book was born in the dark days of the COVID-19 lockdown, when the world seemed to come to a standstill and time was available to put pen to paper.

I would like to thank my beloved Elizabethe Plante for her inspiration and encouragement throughout the process.

I thank RJ Handley and Ky Roase for early support in structure and editing.

I thank Reverend Joshua Reeves for manuscript review and for writing the book's foreword.

I thank Julie Mierau for her editing and proofreading skills, and Maria Robinson for providing the cover design, graphics, and layout.

Finally, I am grateful for my psychology and spiritual teachers throughout the years who provided much of the background for the synthesis of ideas in the book.

Foreword

In spiritual development there is always this seeming bridge to cross—I call it the mystic's bridge—between who we think we are and who we really are, between life as we think it is and life as it really is, between God as we think He is and God as She really is.

This bridge is often alluded to as ego, but it's hard to determine if this ego helps us get to or keeps us from what's truly real.

Few of us can deny that experience where regular modes of thinking break down—spontaneity—and something seems to click or fall into place—synchronicity—and all of a sudden we get who we are, why we are here, and what it all means, if only for a moment—serendipity. There is no clear logical answer in it all, just a true and valid experience of the great mystery of being and becoming.

For the seeker committed to this type of experience, truth becomes the essential goal. Not salvation, not transcendence, just truth, or as Joe Friday used to say on *Dragnet*, "Just the facts." Like a good detective, the seeker follows the truth, wherever it leads. This kind of religion of truth was expressed in the Middle Ages by Meister Eckhart, who said, "What is truth? The truth is something so noble that if God could turn aside from it, I could keep truth and let God go." Or take a more modern religious and political figure such as Mohandas Gandhi, who proclaimed his religion was truth. The right religion is the one, the none, or the many that get you to the truth.

Which leaves us not with the term ego—what Kelly Beninga refers to as "our I"—but what the ego points us to. What is this function of self-awareness? And if not its quest for truth, then for clarity? Clarity of self, clarity of purpose, clarity of reason? Beninga does the bold thing here and does not discriminate against wisdom. He synthesizes wisdom of science, religion, psychology, and philosophy—and doesn't leave himself out of the pondering. What comes together is both refreshingly clear and a relief.

In pop spirituality the ego has unfortunately become a kind of boogeyman within: something we are to distrust, not listen to, and pretend to transcend. Beninga challenges that idea. The ego, although needing discernment, is a biological part of who we are. If we understand it, and perhaps even learn to trust it like we might encourage one to follow their heart, it may help us understand ourselves and become greater vehicles for understanding life all around us.

Beninga's wonderful work here adds him to the long—but unfortunately not long enough—list of real truth seekers, with no agenda but just that: the truth. May this book, rich with study, thoughtfulness, and clarity, bring us all a little bit closer.

Josh Reeves
Lead Minister
Mile Hi Church, Lakewood, Colorado

Introduction

The Enlightened Ego reaches for the core of what it means to be a human being. Evolutionary biology teaches us that we are simply a highly evolved and sophisticated primate.

Spiritual teachers contend that we are spiritual beings temporarily inhabiting these human bodies as a required course in the school of spiritual development. Are we just living out our biological imperatives or is there a deeper meaning to our time on Earth? Is the fact that we are capable of self-reflection about our true nature just another step in our biological evolution or are we on the verge of a breakthrough to a new level of consciousness?

The Enlightened Ego provides a stepping-stone toward revealing the meaning and purpose of the human experience. The goal of this book is to bridge the worlds of science and spirituality regarding human nature. We will examine the motivations behind our hopes, fears, and behaviors, and support the reader in transcending painful contracted patterns. The *ego*, that little understood mysterious force inside each of us, is the central topic we will explore in this pursuit of understanding our true nature.

Whether defined by Sigmund Freud or modern-day spiritual gurus, the term ego has become a chameleon, taking on whatever meaning the user wishes to impress on it. The idea that humans have an ego has become ubiquitous in modern culture, yet what the ego is and why we have one remains a mystery to most. While psychology and human biology have gradually found tentacles of connection over the last century, the ego has largely escaped scientific scrutiny.

For thousands of years, spiritual teachers have attempted to help followers transcend the ego on the path to enlightenment, but exactly what they are transcending remains somewhat of a black box of various opinions and ideas.

Despite what many of us might believe, the ego is not an elusive adversary hell bent on keeping us out of heaven. In fact, the ego provides a clear and vital function for humanity's journey on planet Earth. This function can be understood from a rational, scientific point of view and therefore appreciated for what it is: the single most important factor in what makes us human and the driving force in determining our future as a species.

The best way to understand the ego is through the lens of evolution. This is because our ego is not an accident. It evolved along with our brains to advance the survival and reproductive success of our fragile human bodies in the harsh environments of our evolutionary history. Through natural selection, the collection of thought processes and emotions we typically attribute to the ego evolved to maximize our evolutionary fitness.

The ego adheres to the harsh mathematics of survival and reproduction. The ego cares nothing about human happiness or suffering, other than as tools to reach its evolutionary purpose. Left to the devices of the ego, we are destined for a life dominated by fear, defensiveness, selfishness, and greed, with happiness being only a transitory reward for reaching our subconscious evolutionary goals. These ego traits were critical for protection from danger, for gathering the resources needed for survival, for negotiating tribal societies, for mate selection, and for child rearing. They were required for survival in our hunter-gatherer evolutionary past, and they remain with us today. The genes of those who were not successful in these tasks were lost to the trash heap of evolutionary history.

As long as we are humans inhabiting this planet, our egos are indispensable. We are bonded to them for better or for worse. Conventional psychology is almost entirely dedicated to improving our ego, or personality, to enhance functioning in all aspects of life. Common psychological issues such as anxiety and depression, as well as relationship problems, can be traced back to the ego and wounds to our sense of self. Working through these past wounds and releasing painful emotions is necessary and important to leading a successful life.

Attempting to disregard these egoic wounds in the name of transcendence is a form of spiritual bypassing. However, only focusing on egoic wounds still leaves us ignorant of our true nature. So how does one contend with psychological wounds while also following the path of transcendence to enlightenment?

The path presented in this book embraces the whole self, which encompasses both our egoic self and higher self, in service to personal and spiritual growth. By acknowledging our egoic tendencies on a day-to-day basis, we can recognize that ego is an illusion and not the whole truth of who we are. Striking a balance between these two selves propels us toward true personal and spiritual growth. We can acknowledge and then transcend our ego to live life from an enlightened state of being.

This book draws on the fields of neuroscience and evolutionary psychology to examine the ego from a scientific point of view and shows how the ego serves a useful purpose in the survival and continued evolution of mankind. The ego evolved to provide a function in support of the survival and reproduction of our human bodies, very much like any other bodily function. *The Enlightened Ego* puts the ego in perspective as a necessary tool for physical existence. Viewing the ego from a scientific perspective facilitates the dissolution of many fears, superstitions, and misunderstandings that plague our comprehension of human nature.

After examining the ego through the lens of science, *The Enlightened Ego* then draws on the fields of transpersonal psychology and spirituality to explore how human experience can in fact transcend ego. Our egos do not encompass the whole of human experience. Many spiritual seekers have found a path beyond the ego, one that embraces a more expansive self that can escape the egoic trance. Beyond the ego lies a higher self that can see through the illusion of separation and from which we can live life with unconditional love and in unity with all living beings. The path to enlightenment does not repress or deny the ego, but instead integrates the ego's purpose into our realization of the larger truth.

The Enlightened Ego catches the wave of enlightenment initiated by modern spiritual visionaries such as Eckhart Tolle, Adyashanti, Tara Broch, and Jack Kornfield. While these teachers clearly transcended ego and are exemplary spiritual leaders, they typically do not have scientific backgrounds and speak of the ego in general terms without a clear definition.

The view of ego from the perspective of neuroscience and evolutionary psychology is an advance in the field of psychology and will be of interest to practitioners in the field, regardless of their spiritual orientation. Followers of the contemporary spiritual New Thought movement will gain a deeper understanding of their ego from *The Enlightened Ego* and therefore have deeper insight into their human nature and the path of transcendence that lies before them.

Kelly Beninga

THE ENLIGHTENED EGO

Discover
Your Ego's Purpose
and the
Path of Transcendence

Humanity's Inner Conflict

Two souls, alas, are
housed within my breast,
and each will wrestle
for the mastery there.

Johann Wolfgang von Goethe
1806

> The tribe migrated from Africa as part of the first wave of Homo sapiens to enter the European continent.

In the waning years of the last Ice Age, they struggle to adapt to the cold environment and short winter days of their new northern homeland. As winter approaches, the tribal chief realizes they lack the provisions to sustain them through the long cold winter months. He hatches a plan to raid a nearby tribe that has been catching fish in the river and drying them for winter. For Seth, the chief's teenage son, this will be his first raid. He is both excited and scared as the men prepare their spears and clubs for the daring nighttime robbery.

Their stealthy raid in the dark proves successful, and the warriors fill their leather sacks with a bounty of dried fish. But as the marauders steal away into the night, barking dogs alert the rival tribe to their presence. The rival warriors chase and attack. A surge of adrenaline courses through young Seth's body as he battles a teenage boy from the rival tribe. Seth puts into practice all the battle maneuvers his father taught him. With his superior skills, he soon finds his spear piercing the heart of his opponent.

As his opponent breathes his last breath, Seth catches a reflection of himself in his rival's eyes. Seth is flooded with both the elation of victory in battle and sadness from taking a human life just like his own. The next day, the tribe celebrates the victory and heaps praise on Seth for his bravery in battle. Seth feels the pride of his accomplishment yet cannot seem to shake the image of his vanquished opponent's eyes as he died. It feels almost as if part of Seth died with him.

Seth's inner conflict between taking necessary action to survive versus the concern and connection he felt with another living being feels familiar to many of us. In our modern society, these inner conflicts often take on a more sophisticated tone. We want to give generously to the charities we believe in but want to save money for our own needs. We become anxious when a beloved colleague at the office suddenly becomes a competitor for a promotion. We feel compassion for refugees fleeing persecution and now suffering on our border, but we also feel protective of our country's jobs and resources.

Competing priorities reach into our important relationships. We feel a desire for openness and vulnerability with others yet feel an aversion from fear and distrust of their motives. We want to be kind to our spouse's opposite-sex friend, but a fearful, protective instinct holds us back. Sometimes, we feel as if there are two of us: the instinctual, defensive self that is distrustful and opportunistic, and our higher self that is loving and concerned for the welfare of others. Most of this inner conflict plays out subconsciously, resulting in a vague sense of confusion and uneasiness.

Further, this tendency to prioritize self-interest extends to our intra-psychic world. We feel defensive when someone challenges our ideas and decisions. We feel shame and anger when someone makes a joke at our expense. We are fearful and judgmental of those who do not look, think, and act like us. It's not only physical survival and competition for resources at play. Our carefully crafted sense of self, our self-image of being good and capable can be threatened by those around us.

Why is it so important to defend our self-image? What really is it that we are defending?

If we take a step back and look at our situation in this physical existence, we see that we are in a tough spot. We must kill and ingest other living organisms—plants or animals—to survive. Our fragile bodies must be kept within a narrow temperature range despite rapid variations in weather. We instinctively use violence to defend ourselves against attack by predatory animals or threatening humans. We seldom think about these difficult circumstances because they are just the waters we swim in. We know no other way of living.

At the same time, many of us feel a calling to connect with something greater than ourselves. We feel an invisible and ineffable connection with all of humankind and other living beings. We feel a desire to accomplish something for the greater good of humanity in our time here on Earth. We have a sense there is a universal intelligence or consciousness that rises above all the human drama. These higher callings are often what provide meaning to our lives.

So what forces are we dealing with when we feel the tension between the desire to be generous and unconditionally loving versus the need to prioritize our own self-interest? Psychologists and religious leaders often point to the *ego* as the culprit in our fearful and selfish tendencies. However, just what the ego is and how it plays out in our lives remains a mystery to most. While many phenomena once shrouded in mystery and misconception have become clear under the light of science, the ego largely has escaped scientific scrutiny. Without a clear understanding of what constitutes the ego and its purpose, we are susceptible to confusion, guilt, and shame about our egoic propensities.

The ego serves a useful purpose in the survival and continued evolution of humankind. The ego, like any bodily function, evolved to support the survival and reproduction of our bodies. However, the human story does not end there. Our egos do not encompass the whole of human experience. We can transcend ego and embrace our eternal spiritual self as our guide for our time on Earth.

Seth's inner conflict, as well as our own, is born out of the contentious juxtaposition of our drive for survival and some higher calling. This conflict can be resolved by bringing the true nature of ego out of the darkness and into the light for all to see clearly. With this new knowledge, an integrated approach to balance our egoic existence with our desire to live in universal love and interconnection is possible.

Understanding the nature and purpose of the ego can release much of the fear, guilt, and shame we often associate with our ego and its selfish, protective tendencies. Putting the ego into context provides the opportunity to move beyond its constraints to live a loving, peaceful life.

Darwin's Ego

I have called this principle,
by which each slight
variation, if useful, is
preserved, by the term
of "Natural Selection."

Charles Darwin
1859

The term *ego* was first used in the
English language by John Dewey
(an American educator, psychologist,
and political reformer) in an
article written in 1894 entitled
"The Ego as Cause."

In the article, he states that "the ego is an efficient cause of volition," pointing to the ego as a basis for motivating behavior.

The word "ego" is simply the Latin word for "I." It was Sigmund Freud who popularized the term with his 1923 book *The Ego and the Id*. In it, Freud divided the psyche into three parts: id, superego and ego. In Freud's model, the id is the primitive/instinctual part of the psyche that contains sexual and aggressive drives, and the superego operates as a moral conscience. Freud thought of the ego as the rational part of the mind that mediates between the id and the superego.

While Freud's theory of the psyche had no scientific basis and has largely been discredited today, the term *ego* has stuck with us and is still used in many different contexts. The definition of ego in today's world actually aligns more with John Dewey's original meaning of the ego as an agent of motivation, rather than with Freud's idea of the ego as a mediator between the id and superego.

The Roots of Ego

To truly understand the ego, we must travel a little further back in time to discover the scientific roots of the concept. In 1871, Charles Darwin shared his theories on human evolution and sexual selection in *The Descent of Man* and *Selection in Relation to Sex,* followed in 1872 by *The Expression of the Emotions in Man and Animals.* These books took Darwin's groundbreaking theory of evolution and applied it to human emotions and behavior. Darwin identified emotions as an adaptation to promote evolutionary fitness, no different from any physical trait brought about by evolution.

In Darwin's view, our emotions are a result of natural selection. They developed to enhance survival and reproduction, just like any feature that evolved to provide a competitive edge. In Darwin's theory, emotions were biological functions that persisted because of their inherent usefulness.

While Darwin did not use the term *ego,* his work laid the foundation for understanding the origins of our thoughts, emotions, and behavior. For these functions to exist, they must have been useful (adaptive) in the environment in which humans evolved. In Darwin's theory of evolution, as in today's field of evolutionary psychology, no trait exists unless it has been adaptive. That is to say, no characteristic exists unless it has contributed to the central goals of survival and reproduction. People who survive to a reproductive age and support their children in doing the same will ensure their genes are passed on to future generations. Those individuals who do not reproduce run into an evolutionary dead-end and their genes are lost.

This brutal arithmetic applies to genes for both physical and mental characteristics. The bundle of brain-centered mental traits, such as abstract thought and emotions, are not only needed for survival but are central to what it means to be human. They have evolved to become critical to the continued success of humankind.

While Darwin's theories pointed to a scientific explanation of human psyche and ego, it was a road not taken by his contemporaries. Darwin and Freud corresponded on many topics of mutual interest, but Freud was not a fan of the theory of evolution. Freud referred to Darwin about twenty times in various publications but never endorsed the idea of natural selection.

As the field of psychology took off at the beginning of the twentieth century, dominated by behaviorism and Freud's psychoanalytic theories, Darwin's evolutionary view of emotions died out. In an ironic application of "survival of the fittest" to ideas, Freud's original definition of ego has little meaning in today's field of psychology and a clear definition remains elusive. This has created an opportunity for Darwin's ideas on emotionality to be applied to the ego. Because even in today's technological world, just what the ego is and does remains somewhat of a mystery.

To fill the void, religion and culture co-opted the term ego and assigned various meanings to it. In Eastern religions, ego is seen as the root of all human suffering and an obstacle to living a spiritual life. In Western religions, the ego is seen as our sinful self which must be overcome in order to be "saved" or accepted by God. The selfish tendencies of the ego are a source of fear, guilt, and shame for many of those from a religious background.

In popular culture, people with a big ego are thought to have an inflated opinion of themselves. The ego is often seen as some dark force controlling our behavior against our conscious will. It's as if a ghost resides within us, out of our control, with destructive intentions buried in the subconscious.

What Is Ego?

In modern psychological systems, the ego is generally defined as the separate sense of self with a tendency to prioritize our own self-interests and defend ourselves against challenges. The ego is the mind-centered self that contains our thoughts and feelings in an organized structure. It also observes these functions to pass judgment on their legitimacy to ourselves and to others. While this definition provides a general idea of what the ego does, why and how the ego functions has not been clear.

We can turn to the modern field of evolutionary psychology for a clearer picture of the true nature of our ego. Evolutionary psychology is built on the foundation of Darwin's work in the social and natural sciences. This field examines the psychological and behavioral evolutionary adaptations that produced the mental processes of modern humans. Researchers investigate the psychological traits that are the result of natural or sexual selection in human evolution. Genetic mutations of the brain that contribute to fitness for survival are "selected" and passed on to the next generation. Over millions of years, evolution has given humans sophisticated mental advantages for survival and reproduction in the dangerous and competitive environment of our planet.

The drive for survival and reproduction is the basis for the ego. The ego is not a mystery. It is neither good nor bad. It just is. The ego is necessary equipment for survival in the realm of physical existence. Our brains evolved to maximize our chances to pass our genes on to the next generation. As Darwin posited, evolution produced our mental abilities, including complex thinking and planning, emotional responses, and the ability to create social bonds. All the qualities we typically assign to the ego can be traced back to the basic human drive for survival and reproduction.

Life and death are inextricably linked. Animals need a continuous source of calories and nutrition to survive, which requires the death of other living organisms. Being "naked apes," we humans must protect our bodies from the elements with clothing and shelter. For much of our existence, acquiring food, clothing, and shelter has been our top priority for daily survival. These resources often are limited in our environment. This sets up a competitive environment, both with other humans and other species.

All living beings have finite lifetimes. Passing on our genes to future generations requires not only survival but also reproduction. In fact, on the unconscious biological level, reproduction is the ultimate goal of all humans. Without reproduction, our genetic traits will not be passed on, and any genetic mutations that contribute to fitness for survival would be lost. This drive can often be seen in the highly protective behavior of parents toward their children. From an evolutionary perspective, survival of our offspring is more important than our own survival.

Newborn babies are in a pre-egoic state of helplessness until they develop the ability to defend themselves, both mentally and physically. These defenses require the ability to distinguish between friend or foe, to alert parents when in danger, and to develop social bonds with family and tribal members. Children have to develop an ego to survive to child-bearing age and to pass their genes onto the next generation. The ego is not optional. It is essential equipment for success.

Humans are the most highly evolved animal on the planet. We dominate the planet today because our ancestors evolved complex social structures to enhance resource gathering and defense on the tribal level, as well as to provide opportunities for mating and reproduction. From the evolutionary viewpoint, acquiring more power and resources increases the chances of our genes surviving to another generation.

In our modern society, money is the ultimate symbol of power and resources. The amount of time and effort modern humans put into acquiring money is a testament to this basic survival and reproductive instinct. These biological drives align well with the typical definition of the ego and explain why the ego exists. In the next chapter, we will explore aspects of the ego from the view of neuroscience and evolutionary psychology in more detail.

CH3

The Biological Basis for Ego

The separation of psychology from the premises of biology is purely artificial, because the human lives in indissoluble union with the body.

Carl Jung
1937

The mental characteristics that promote survival and reproduction need some sort of organizational agent in order to provide a sense of self.

The ego evolved to fulfill this vital function. How we develop this sense of self is best understood from the perspective of neurobiology. Understanding our ego from this scientific perspective helps dispel prevalent misconceptions and superstitions about the ego and opens a window into seeing our true nature beyond ego.

How We Perceive the World

As we turn toward defining the neurological basis for the organization of ego, let us first look at how the human brain evolved to create consciousness. We typically do not give much thought to how we perceive and define the world around us—or ourselves for that matter. Beyond our field of awareness, a complex neurological process is working on our behalf. We have five senses to take in information from the environment (sight, sound, smell, taste, touch). These five senses can be thought of as peripheral instruments collecting data for input to our central processor, our brain. These five senses are all we have to perceive our surroundings.

In actuality, these information-gathering instruments are somewhat limited. They evolved for reasons of survival rather than for providing an accurate depiction of the multilayered richness of reality. For example, our eyes can only discern light in the wavelength range of 400 to 700 nanometers from an available range of ten to 10,000 nanometers. Human eyesight, hearing, and smell are inferior to some other species that evolved to have more acute senses.

There is also a whole range of physical phenomena we are incapable of perceiving at all. Some animals are capable of discerning magnetic fields, which they use for navigation. Large frequency ranges of electromagnetic radiation are useful for communication services such as radios, mobile phones, and GPS, yet cannot be detected by the human body. We are simply unaware of much of the physical phenomena around us. This is because human evolution "decided" that this extraneous information is unnecessary for our survival. There is much more information available to us than we can process, and evolution gave us an efficient filter so our brains are not overwhelmed.

From neurobiology, we know our five senses take in information from our environment, and our brain creates a model of our world based on this information. This sensory information is received by the *thalamus,* a walnut-shaped mass near the center of the brain, and processed in the *parietal lobe* near the top of the brain. (See Figure 1.) Both this sensory input and data stored in memory are used to create an internal model of our external world. For example, our eyes perceive the colors green and brown in the general outline of branches and a trunk. Our memory banks will recall similar data and project the remaining details of the object to create an image of a tree in the parietal lobe. Hence, we do not actually "see" the tree. We take in a limited amount of data with our senses and create a mental image of the tree in our brains, which may or may not be accurate. It is not reality itself, but instead is a mind-generated image of reality. The model of the world created by our brains is limited by the information humans can actually perceive.

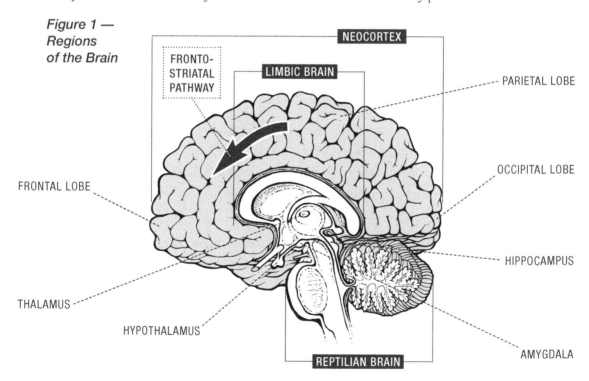

Figure 1 —
Regions
of the Brain

What's more, to reduce the amount of information processed, our brain will focus on the aspects of our environment that are most important for our well-being. Other data gathered through our senses is discarded as irrelevant. Imagine a crowded party where your best friend is telling you of an emotional experience. All other voices, sights, and sounds are tuned out by your brain as you hang on her every word.

How Self-Image Is Created

A modeling process like the one used in defining the world around us is used to create our self-image. A neurodynamic tool evolved in the brain to create this self-image. This inner tool has been termed the *Phenomenal Self Model* (PSM). The PSM is a distinct organizational structure and pattern of neural activity that integrates thoughts, feelings, and memories into an image of our-selves. The PSM is created over time as our brain structures are activated by our environment. The PSM is primarily located in the *frontal lobe* of the brain. The PSM is somewhat modifiable based on learning new information and by the environment we are in from moment to moment.

From the perspective of the individual, we are unable to realize that our sense of self is simply the content of this simulation in our brain. From our naïve state of experience day to day, the PSM becomes the structure for our ego. We typically take the PSM as reality, just as we take the created image of the world around us as reality. We become conscious when our brains successfully create this unified and dynamic inner portrait of reality, with the image of ourselves at the center of the image of our external surroundings.

This internal image is the ego, or self, as it appears in conscious experience. Just as with our perception of our environment, it is not a self in reality but rather a brain-generated image of self. The ego is not a nebulous, unknown force inside our head. The center of the brain-generated blueprint of reality is what we experience as ourselves, the ego. We are inherently unable to recog-nize that all this is just the content of a simulation in our brain. This unconsciousness of the PSM on our part is what makes the PSM our ego. We see the world and ourselves from the perspective of our ego. We do not see our ego—we see with it.

From an individual's perspective, our self-image, or ego, feels like it is "us." But no such thing as self as we imagine it exists in physical reality. Just as a computer-generated model of an object is not the object itself, our brain-generated image of self is not an actual self. A collection of neural networks in a biological organism is not a true self. What we experience as self, or ego, is merely a model in our brain.

The Purpose of Ego

The function of the ego is to organize our subjective experience into a sense of self. The ego is an efficient device to allow humans to consciously conceive of ourselves and our place in the world. But what is this subjective experience that makes up the contents of the ego? An inclusive model of the ego contains all of human experience: perceptions, emotions, thoughts, mental images, instincts, impulses, desires, and memories. These are the building blocks that make up the PSM and, ultimately, our ego. These building blocks are constantly interacting with each other and our environment to create our subjective experience on a moment-to-moment basis.

So, what is the purpose of our ego and how does it function? What is really going on inside our ego structure, the PSM? To answer these questions, we need to return to the central thesis that the ego contains our evolved mental equipment for survival and reproduction. If we cannot survive and reproduce, our genes are eliminated from the gene pool. The ego contains all the mental tools necessary to maximize our chances of survival and reproduction in the environment for which it evolved. All of the typical human thoughts, emotions, and actions can be traced back to this basic goal. Our fragile human bodies need constant protection and nourishment. The ego diligently sets about this task, both on a moment-to-moment basis and in planning for our future survival. This function of the ego is best understood from the viewpoint of evolutionary psychology.

In our 200 million years of evolution as mammals, and five million years of evolution as humans, we evolved with basic survival and reproduction strategies appropriate for a culture of hunters-gatherers in a dangerous environment where death was a real possibility on a day-to-day basis. Until about the year 1900, the average lifespan of humans was only about thirty years. To survive to a reproductive age and care for young children, humans evolved to become risk averse. Our mental and physical efforts were focused on obtaining resources, protecting us from danger, and obtaining suitable mates. Humans did not evolve to achieve our highest potential. Rather, we evolved simply to pass our genes on to the next generation.

Evolution has preprogrammed us to avoid danger whenever possible. This risk aversion plays out in what is called *negativity bias,* where we unconsciously look for the worst-case scenario in each situation. In our evolutionary past, assuming that there was a lion behind every rock paid off if there actually was a lion behind one in 100 rocks. Therefore, people with a higher negativity bias had a higher chance of survival.

Fear plays an inordinate role in our ego makeup because fear is the primary tool with which our ego supports our physical survival. Fear makes us alert to potential dangers and engages our bodies' sympathetic nervous system to prepare for fight or flight. Without fear, the lifespan of all mammals, including humans, would be quite brief. From the perspective of ego, fear is a much more critical emotion than happiness. An almond-shaped structure termed the *amygdalae* is our brain's watchdog and is constantly scanning for threats around us. It will sound the fear alarm whenever anything seems amiss. Our ego evolved to promote survival and reproduction with the absolute minimum of risk. Therefore, our egos will bias us toward the status quo with an aversion to any risky endeavors. Any situation that is unfamiliar will cause our ego to retract out of fear.

In primitive societies, possession of resources such as food, clothing, shelter, tools, weapons, and livestock were signs of wealth and power. Such resources not only improved the chances of survival but were attractive to potential mates who could use them to both ensure their own survival and increase the chances that their offspring would reach a reproductive age. The possession of resources became a status symbol of fitness for survival and reproduction. The chiefs or leaders of tribes typically had the largest cache of resources and the greatest access to sexual partners. Obtaining resources demanded risk-taking behaviors, such as hunting dangerous animals, traveling away from tribal settlements to gather food, and battling with rival tribes for territory, resources, and mates. This inner conflict between risk aversion and risk-taking to acquire resources in the form of money still plays out in our egos today.

In hunter-gatherer societies living close to the land and dependent on its resources, survival depends not only on personal safety and resource possession but also on the well-being of the tribe as a whole and on the strength of social connections within the tribe. Members of the tribe with the best social connections are most likely to be protected from danger and given resources from others when needed. Power is measured not only by resource possession but also by the ability to influence others to act in our benefit. Social bonds with family and other tribal members were required to successfully provide defense against outside threats, acquire mates, and raise offspring to a reproductive age.

Ego Development

As the son of the tribal chief, Seth was born into privilege, as his father controlled many resources and held the highest social position in the tribe. Seth was provided particular attention in training for hunting, fighting, and other tasks expected of men in the tribe. Both his parents were attentive to his needs, and he was well-liked within the tribe. He was in a good position to take over as the tribal chief when the time came. Seth had his eye on the most beautiful young women in the tribe, who reciprocated his interest. His evolutionary fitness from his privileged start in life was shown when he vanquished his opponent in the raid of the neighboring tribe, who likely did not have the same resources and training as Seth.

Human infants are born in an immature state and take a long time to reach maturity compared to other species. This demands both a high investment in time and resources from parents and a high level of infant dependency on parents for survival and socialization. All mammal young develop a special bond with their mothers to maximize the chances of survival. An innate function in the brain of human infants promotes safety by establishing this bond with our mothers. When the mother is absent, the infant feels distress and produces a signal cry in an attempt to reestablish safety. Mother and child are mutually attuned and seek the other out when the child is hungry, frightened, or in pain. Mothers must be consistently responsive to infants for this attachment to take place. This is our first experience with developing trust in our earthly environment.

The field of study concerning the development of these attachments is called *Attachment Theory,* which has become important in the research and therapy of both childhood and adult relationships. The quality of attachment to a parent or primary caregiver in childhood sets up a template for all future relationships. A healthy childhood attachment leads to the development of a healthy ego that promotes survival, pair bonding, bonds with family and other tribal members, and child rearing. A poor attachment to parents, such as when a young child is orphaned, leads to poor functioning in relationships as an adult. Poor attachments may also lead to low self-esteem and lack of confidence in survival fitness. Therefore, healthy attachments promote the purposes of the ego in passing our genes on to future generations.

Another important development in human socialization is the specialization of skills that allow tribal members to become proficient at certain tasks while trading goods and services with those of other specializations. As culture evolved, this social structure became more complex, to the benefit of all societal members. From the perspective of ego, these cooperative efforts are ultimately in one's self-interest and are an unconscious quid pro quo. We unconsciously expect to benefit more from societal cooperation than we would from a go-it-alone approach.

As anthropologists discovered, there is an interplay between biological evolution and cultural evolution. Just as the human genome has evolved, so has the cultural environment. Our human culture evolves first, and our biological evolution plays catch-up to try to adapt appropriately to the cultural environment. Researchers conclude that many cultural changes in the Holocene period (that is the last 10,000 years), such as the domestication of animals and plants and the rise of high-density human settlements, exerted selection pressures to which the human genome responded. This suggests that humans, by altering the world through agriculture, villages, architecture, and social institutions, shape our own evolution to a significant degree. However, human evolution through natural selection is a painstakingly slow process. At best, modern humans are biologically better adapted to the agrarian society of the last few thousand years than our modern technological society.

Some readers may find this biological basis for ego to be highly reductionistic and may even be offended by the idea that our sense of self is simply a brain-based simulation resulting from evolutionary imperatives. Indeed, this discussion addresses humanity as a homogeneous group and does not include a discussion of the minor differences in individuals resulting from unique combinations of inherited genes and from genetic mutations. The childhood environment also plays a substantial role in the formation of each unique personality. While these factors contribute to the richness of human variety, the basic functioning of the ego is much the same throughout humanity.

In summary, our egos are a biologically based assembly of brain functions meant to facilitate survival and reproduction. The functions of the ego are organized into an image of ourselves, or PSM, as a means of providing a coherent system to formulate a sense of "us" and our location in the world. In this chapter we have defined the structure and function of the ego from the viewpoint of neurobiology. In Chapter 4, we will explore the contents and operation of the ego in our daily lives.

CH4

The Ego in Action

Your emotions are the
slaves to your thoughts,
and you are the slave
to your emotions.

Elizabeth Gilbert
2006

We humans tend to think of
ourselves as the sum total of our
thoughts and emotions.

Indeed, thoughts and emotions make up the vast majority of our internal experience, and it is easy to make the assumption that they encompass our identity. However, thoughts and emotions are simply biological brain functions that have evolved to assure our survival and reproduction. Realizing this perspective can be unsettling and challenge long-held beliefs about ourselves. Facing the truth about the purpose of our ego, including the function of thoughts and emotions, creates an opportunity to disidentify with ego and begin an exploration of the true self that exists beyond ego.

Components of Ego

Emotions are often the direct result of external stimuli, such as a wild animal attack that elicits fear and the fight-or-flight response, or the affection felt from the smile of a loved one. However, along with humans' unique capacity for abstract thought came the ability to generate emotions from a preceding thought. We frequently have a thought/judgment and then experience an emotion based on the thought. For example, one might read a news article about crime in their neighborhood, have the thought that their own home is in danger, and experience fear as a result. The entire process occurs in a matter of seconds and typically beyond our conscious awareness.

Emotions can generally be divided into two categories: aversions and attractions. Aversions are painful emotions meant to inhibit behavior or cause avoidance of dangerous situations. Attractions are pleasant emotions meant to motivate behavior that supports evolutionary fitness. In service of survival, painful aversive emotions can dominate much of our experience.

We can further break down the function of the ego by looking at its attributes and discerning the evolutionary purpose of each component. Table 1 shows a list of ego attributes and their functions in regard to survival and reproduction. These ego attributes are based on research in the field of evolutionary psychology. For example, happiness is only a temporary state meant to provide a short-term reward for achievement of goals that contribute to evolutionary fitness. From the ego's perspective, a continuous state of happiness would promote complacency and would inhibit further efforts to reach additional goals. Therefore, ongoing happiness is counter to the purpose of the ego. Happiness is just one tool of the ego out of many meant to promote survival and reproduction. The ego places no value judgment on whether an emotion is painful or pleasurable. Emotions are only useful to inhibit or promote behavior in the service of evolutionary fitness.

From the egoic perspective, even love has the utilitarian purpose of creating bonds between family and tribal members to promote survival. Passionate love between partners furthers reproductive goals by cementing the pair bond long enough to produce and raise children. Egoic love is an unconscious bargain, with a beneficial return expected from our investment of time and resources into the loved one.

Altruistic behavior toward non-kin can at times appear as unconditional or selfless love, seemingly at odds with evolutionary theory. From the view of evolutionary psychology, such behavior will only occur if there is a chance for reciprocity at a later time or if such behavior can improve one's status with potential mates or other tribal members. This is not to say unconditional love does not exist; it's just that it does not exist in the world of the ego. At times it may be difficult to discern between true non-egoic unconditional love and altruistic behavior that appears unconditional but in actuality anticipates a future benefit toward evolutionary fitness to the provider.

Table 1 — Ego Attributes and Their Evolutionary Purpose

EGO ATTRIBUTE	EVOLUTIONARY PURPOSE
Fear	Alerts to danger and primes the body to take action. Blood supply to the muscles is increased and the mind becomes focused on fighting or finding escape routes. Fear in the form of risk aversion promotes survival by minimizing exposure to dangerous situations. Fears that seem unreasonable and disproportionate are called phobias, which may represent inherited hardwired tendencies to fear certain objects or organisms.
Anger	A protection of perceived mental or physical boundaries. Can provoke violence. Acts of retribution signal to another the cost of provoking anger in this and future situations. Anger may therefore be costly to the actor in the short run but, in the long run, it may be adaptive in modifying future behavior of others.
Sadness	Weakens our motivation to continue with the present course of action. May be a means of telling the person to stop current strategies and conserve resources since they are unrewarding. A sign of lowered self-esteem. Could also be a signal that help is required.
Jealousy	Forces us to be alert to signs of deception by partners. May activate aggressive behaviors to force the defecting partner back to original relationship or deter partner and trespassing partner from continuing in the new relationship.
Love	Love for family members increases cooperation and altruism to promote fitness of the family unit. Passionate love in mating can further reproductive goals by cementing the pair bond long enough to produce and raise children.
Happiness	Provides emotional reward for achieving desired goals that contribute to repro-ductive fitness. Happiness results from obtaining resources, mates, children, or raised social status. Happiness is a temporary state followed by discontentment to motivate achievement of additional goals.
Disgust	Initiates avoidance of potentially dangerous situations. Disgust is also the fear of ingesting an undesirable substance. Sexual disgust with family serves to inhibit inbreeding.
Guilt	Remorseful feeling that follows self-awareness of having been unfair to family or tribal members. May serve to drive more cooperative or generous behavior in future encounters to promote reciprocal cooperative behavior.
Anxiety	A combination of fear and desire. Provides motivation to avoid an undesired out-come and to pursue a desired outcome.
Self-esteem	Provides a self-measure of fitness for survival and reproduction. Low self-esteem is subconsciously linked to potential death, either physical or genetic, and is therefore highly anxiety provoking.
Defensiveness	Mitigates fear and anxiety resulting from perceived threats to survival fitness (self-esteem) by providing rationalizations against failure and outside negative judgments.

EGO ATTRIBUTE	EVOLUTIONARY PURPOSE
Competitiveness	Promotes success against competitors for acquisition of resources, mates, or social status. Wining temporarily raises self-esteem.
Greed	Driving force for acquisition of money and resources, sometimes beyond what is needed for survival and attraction of suitable mates.
Thoughts	Thoughts about the present help to evaluate the most effective action in each situation. Thoughts about the past or future provide the ability to learn from past experience and plan for success in the future. Thoughts may be distorted by limited sensory perception and cognitive dissonance.
Negativity Bias	Propensity to think of and act on the worst-case scenario in any situation. Promotes survival by biasing awareness and action toward potential danger.
Memories	Short-term and long-term memory serve to store relevant information for later recall in the service of dealing with dangerous situations, creating social bonds, acquiring resources, mating, and child rearing. Brain plasticity in youth adapts to the local environment for optimum fitness.
Need to Control	Controlling thoughts and behaviors are an attempt to exert power over others in order to manipulate them to act in a way that is beneficial to the controller. A sense of control can also temporarily mitigate fear and serve as an ego defense.
Need to Be Right	Self-judgments that we are right and convincing others we are right raises self-esteem and perceived social status. Being proven wrong lowers self-esteem.

Our Brain and Ego

The human brain is roughly divided into three sections: the reptilian brain, the limbic brain, and the neocortex. (See Figure 1.) The evolution of these brain sections is in the order shown. Each section evolved with ever more sophisticated capabilities to promote survival. The reptilian brain is primarily occupied with operating the peripheral autonomic nervous system—the regulation of vital senses and organs. The limbic brain is primarily involved in generating emotions to motivate or discourage behavior. The *amygdala* as well as the *hypothalamus, thalamus,* and *hippocampus* are all contained within the limbic brain and each has a role in generating emotions. The neocortex was the last to develop and is the seat of reasoning and logical thought. Our ability to plan for the future and use language are based in the neocortex.

The emotions shown in Table 1 are all generated within the limbic brain, which induces the secretion of a cocktail of various hormones and neurotransmitters to create the appropriate emotion. The limbic brain does not have the ability to discern between imaginary representations generated by the neocortex and perceptions of the actual environment. Therefore, emotions will be generated by the limbic brain regardless of whether we are reacting to actual events in our environment or to neocortex-generated thoughts and images. This characteristic of the limbic brain is easily demonstrated by watching a suspenseful movie, where our limbic brain generates emotions as if the situation were real and happening in the present moment. Because our limbic brain cannot discern between real events and imagination, our emotions often have little or no basis in reality. This is an important point for later discussion.

The last nine ego items in Table 1 are reactions primarily initiated in the neocortex, requiring cognitive reasoning or thoughts to carry out their function. Thoughts and emotions for these items occur in an interactive loop, feeding off of each other to create the egoic reaction. Usually a neocortex-based thought results in a limbic brain-based fear, which leads to more defensive thoughts. Together, the functions shown in the table create the contents of the ego, organized into the PSM, as discussed earlier. The ego is both our self-image and the tools it contains for survival and reproduction.

Self-Esteem as a Measure of Fitness

Humans have an unconscious and continuous desire to measure our success in acquiring resources, finding suitable mates, and producing offspring. This desire is also an evolved trait because we need data feedback to discern our fitness for survival and our power/resources compared to competitors. A term that works well to define this fitness feedback mechanism is *self-esteem*. Self-esteem can be defined as a subconscious self-measure of our ability to be successful in survival and reproduction. It is a measure of the effectiveness of our ego. Researchers at Dartmouth College identified a region of the human brain that seems to predict a person's self-esteem levels. It's called the *Frontostriatal Pathway,* and the stronger and more active it is in the brain, the more self-esteem someone has.

In our evolutionary past, low self-esteem was a signal that one was unable to deal effectively with threats such as starvation, attack by enemies, inhospitable climate, or being ostracized by the tribe. From an evolutionary perspective, low self-esteem is akin to a threat of death. Our brains will interpret this perceived inability to achieve our goals as a threat to our very existence. This produces the anxiety and fear that often accompany low self-esteem. In our subconscious, we are judging ourselves to be unfit for survival and reproduction

Of course, we do not consciously think of self-esteem in such basic terms. In our modern society, self-esteem is based on external achievements such as the ability to get an education, climb the corporate ladder, find an attractive mate, have a big house, raise beautiful children, and save for retirement. Having a large circle of admiring friends and colleagues also contributes to raising our self-esteem. Based on our discussion of our biological evolution, it is not a large leap to see how these modern measures of success trace back to the core evolutionary drives for survival and reproduction.

Our self-image is not static. Throughout life, it changes based on our circumstances, know-ledge or skills obtained, and our ability to successfully navigate our environment. Self-esteem is a barometer to measure our perceived ability to be successful in achieving our core drives. People who are seen to have a big ego may just be highly confident in their ability to achieve desired outcomes. This confidence or high self-esteem can come from successful achievements, with each achievement built on the previous one. The opposite is also true, where one failure after another reduces our self-esteem and can lead to learned helplessness and hopelessness. Both high and low self-esteem are self-measures of the ego's efficacy, and either can be distorted in comparison to "reality."

Ego Defenses

When we feel threats to our ego, we are taking in information from our environment that reflects poorly on our ability to achieve the ego's primary drives. In other words, our self-esteem is lowered. Such threats can come from many different sources, such as losing out in a competitive environment, comparing ourselves to others who are more successful, feeling the negative judgments of other people, or failing to achieve an important goal. As our self-esteem is lowered by these circumstances, the positive image (ego) of ourselves is threatened. As previously discussed, the unconscious fear of death by lowered self-esteem can lead to anxiety and depression. To mitigate anxiety in such circumstances, the ego has evolved defenses. The "defensiveness" attribute of ego shown in Table 1 can be further broken into differing types. Sigmund Freud noted a number of ego defenses that he refers to throughout his written works. His daughter, Anna Freud, developed these ideas and elaborated on them, adding ten of her own. Many psychoanalysts have also added further types of ego defenses. The most commonly referenced ego defenses are shown in Table 2.

Table 2 — Ego Defense Mechanisms

DEFENSE MECHANISM	DEFINITION
Displacement	Shifting unacceptable feelings or impulses from the target of those feelings to someone less threatening, or to an object.
Intellectualization	Resorting to excessive abstract thinking rather than focusing on the upsetting aspects of issues that cause conflict or stress.
Reaction Formation	Transforming an unacceptable feeling or desire into its opposite in order to make it more acceptable.
Repression	Unconsciously excluding disturbing emotions, thoughts, or experiences from awareness.
Denial	Dealing with emotional conflict or stress by refusing to acknowledge a painful aspect of reality or experience that would be apparent to others.
Projection	Attributing undesirable personal traits or feelings to someone else to protect one's ego from acknowledging distasteful personal attributes.
Sublimation	Transferring an unacceptable impulse or desire into a socially appropriate activity or interest.
Regression	Dealing with emotional conflict or stress by reverting to childish behaviors.
Rationalization	Explaining an unacceptable behavior or feeling in a rational or logical manner, avoiding the true reason for the behavior.
Disassociation	Becoming separated or removed from one's experience.
Compensation	Overachieving in one area to compensate for failures in another.

While many of Freud's theories have been discredited by modern psychology, his terminology for these ego defenses has remained remarkably resilient in the face of decades of research into human personality. In fact, they are still used in psychotherapy today. Activation of ego defenses comes at a cost. The amount of valuable mental energy consumed by engaging these defenses can only be explained by the existential fear of death underlying them. In our evolutionary past, low self-esteem—the self-judgment that we are unfit for survival and reproduction—actually was a signal that there was a high likelihood of death, either physically or genetically. In modern society, the stakes are not typically so high, but these ego defenses remain in our psyche. Whenever our sense of self is threatened, our defenses against lowered self-esteem are activated.

To summarize, our ego employs various emotions and thought/emotion complexes to further our evolutionary goals. Fear is the predominant emotion of the ego, as this was the key tool to avoid danger and promote survival in our evolutionary history. We perform a self-measure of our ego's effectiveness and fitness, which is called self-esteem. For our brains that developed primarily in dangerous hunter-gatherer environments, low self-esteem is akin to a death threat. Therefore, we developed mental ego defenses to mitigate the fear and anxiety that can accompany low self-esteem.

Our egos evolved in consonance with human evolution to provide the mental software needed to maximize the chances for survival of our physical bodies in hostile environments. We could not survive without it. However, our ego's programming for that singular purpose also creates limitations and obstacles for modern humans who aspire to reach their full potential. We will explore this darker side of ego in the next chapter.

CH5

The Problem with Ego

The ego, however, is not
who you really are. The
ego is your self-image,
it is your social mask, it
is the role you are playing.
Your social mask thrives
on approval. It wants
control, and it is sustained
by power because it lives
in fear.

Ram Dass
1971

As discussed in previous chapters,
our ego serves a vital role on planet
Earth by promoting survival, acquisition
of resources, and reproduction
leading to the continued evolution
of our species.

Any attempts to live without our ego would be met with harsh reality. However, that is not to say the ego does not present considerable obstacles to the higher goals of modern humans, such as long-term happiness and cooperation with our fellow human beings on a planetary level. In this chapter, we will explore some of the modern ego-created problems and obstacles.

Evolved traits that continue to contribute to our fitness for success in our modern society can be called adaptive. Evolved traits that inhibit success in our modern society can be called mal-adaptive. Since we primarily evolved in hunter-gatherer societies, many of the ego traits we carry into today's world are maladaptive to success as we now typically define it. Humans are attempting to adapt to a sophisticated and complex society very different from the one for which we evolved. The results are predictably quite mixed.

Happiness and Fear

From the egoic perspective, happiness is a pleasurable sensation meant to reward goal achievement on a short-term basis, to be followed by discontentment and more ambition to achieve additional goals in the service of evolutionary fitness. The ego employs the proverbial carrot on a stick, compelling us to always want more than we have, with happiness being only a fleeting sensation. With happiness, rather than day-to-day survival, being the primary goal of most modern humans, the ego's sparing use of happiness as a temporary reward system creates quite a problem. Abiding happiness remains elusive to most of us.

By necessity, fear is the predominant emotion that motivates human behavior because it was critical to our survival in our harsh evolutionary past. Although actual death from a dangerous encounter is relatively rare in the modern Western world, our emotional (limbic) brain has not evolved to adapt to modern circumstances. Our limbic brain will generate fear reactions in non-life-threatening situations and whenever our self-esteem is threatened. Because of the negativity bias in our thought process, we imagine potentially dangerous situations and feel fear when oftentimes it is not warranted. This imagination-generated fear, along with our inherent risk aversion, causes us to cling to the status quo rather than pursue goals that may ultimately be in our best interest. This exaggerated fear can also keep us from pursuing relationships and social connections that could lead to increased happiness and satisfaction.

Tilting at Windmills

As outlined in Chapter 3, our ego is an internally generated image of ourselves that contains our survival mechanisms. We provide a self-reflective measure of evolutionary fitness which we define as self-esteem. Any threats to our self-esteem are met with anger and defensiveness. However, this internally generated self-image (ego) is ultimately an illusion and is just a series of brain functions meant to promote survival and reproduction.

Humans spend an inordinate amount of time and mental energy on defensive measures to protect our ego and bolster our self-esteem. From an evolutionary perspective, this must have been an adaptive trait at some point. In today's world, ego defenses generate fear and anxiety that is counter to any conscious goals of happiness and contentment. We are all Don Quixote, battling with windmills that often are no threat to our well-being. Our amplified sense of fear has become maladaptive.

Our egos engage in an unconscious calculus—to maximize the benefit to ourselves while minimizing our giving to others. Selfish behavior is unbecoming when it is overtly apparent, so we often engage in covert manipulation of others to get what we want. Asking directly for what we want often did not work as children, so we learned veiled ways to get what we need. Most of us were manipulated by parents into doing as they wanted. We learned these manipulative techniques well and practice them as adults.

Inducing fear, guilt, shame, and obligation are the preferred tools of the ego to manipulate others. We subtly threaten others with withdrawal of love and attention if we don't get what we want. We make others feel guilty if they don't fulfill our desires. We use fear to enforce unspoken rules when we don't like others' behavior. We expect gratitude and reciprocation when we do give to others. The subconscious goal is to get others to do what we want without us appearing to do so. The end result is pseudo relationships that are not loving, trusting, or fulfilling. Such relationships are held together by a sense of obligation rather true joy and intimacy.

The Mind Trap

The defining trait that sets humans apart from other species is our well-developed neo-cortex that has evolved the capacity to evaluate past events and plan for future ones. Our ability for reasoning and abstract thought has allowed humans to thoroughly dominate all other species and extract great volumes of resources from the planet. We are capable of complex linear and spatial reasoning that has brought about the technological advances of the modern age.

However, our ability for abstract thought, combined with the little-evolved emotional reactions of the limbic brain, has created a mind trap that it is difficult for us to escape. The often-fearful response of the limbic brain to rather benign situations creates unnecessary suffering and sets our neocortex off on a mission to identify and neutralize the source of the fear. This is often a fool's errand, as there is no real danger to locate. The end result is that our minds spin out of control in an attempt to solve a problem that does not exist. Mark Twain was aware of this human characteristic when he quipped: "I am an old man and have known a great many troubles, but most of them never happened."

In our modern society, we usually do not have actual threats to our physical safety and survival. Just the same, our negativity bias will perceive threats where there are none, triggering the activation of ego defenses to defend our egos against threats to our self-esteem. In actuality, our ego is nothing but an illusory image in our brain and there is nothing real to defend. Nonetheless, our neocortex will spin its wheels looking for the source of the threat and create plans to defend ourselves against these imaginary threats.

This is a well-known phenomenon to meditators, who often call this "monkey mind." When our ego is in control, our minds generate endless threatening scenarios, emotional reactions, and defensive plans. We build a list of grievances against others in our minds. This process is rife with fears, judgments, criticisms, and imagined defensive reactions. Our minds often develop a story in which we are superior to others in order to temporarily bolster our self-esteem. Most people are on autopilot and totally unaware of the fact that our thought processes are out of our conscious control. Rather than using our neocortex as a tool for effective planning, it spins out of control with erroneous and useless thoughts. This often results in our limbic brain reacting with fear and anxiety that is seldom necessary or productive.

The ego is a future-oriented device because it is focused on our future survival. Fear and greed are the primary tools the ego uses to keep us forward looking. The ego is obsessed with two general categories of activity: getting things we want but don't have, such as money, power, material possessions, and romantic relationships; and becoming someone who we are not, such as happy, peaceful, wealthy, successful, and famous. The very fact that we see all of these goals in the future and as things we must strive to obtain actually sabotages the possibility of experiencing them in the present.

The ego cannot reside in the present moment. A brief satisfying experience of reaching a goal is immediately replaced by a feeling of inadequacy. We must once again have something else that we do not or be someone else who we are not. From the egoic perspective, guilt and rumination about the past serves the purpose of motivating course correction in the future. Sitting peacefully in the present serves no purpose toward evolutionary fitness. It is wasted time in a nonproductive and vulnerable state. Therefore, the hamster wheel continues to turn, driven by a sense of inadequacy and a never-ending stream of goals we think will finally provide lasting satisfaction.

The Ego and Society

The population density of Earth is currently much greater than in the entirety of human evolution. We live in a highly competitive society with enormous wealth and sociopolitical power concentration. Inequality of resource possession has reached extreme levels. Complex technology plays an outsized role in today's world. Globalization and environmental destruction have forced us to confront issues on a global scale, rather than just addressing local issues impacting our community. Wealth depends on a complex economy over which most individuals have little control. Many features of modern economies, such as office work, research and development, education, job markets, and factory work require larger delays between investment and payoff compared to the hunting and gathering cultures in which we evolved.

Most citizens of developed nations possess far more money and resources than anyone throughout evolutionary history, and our physical survival faces relatively few risks. Our propensity for behavior primarily motivated by fear and greed is maladaptive in many modern situations. Our fear, risk aversion, and drive for resource attainment results in missed opportunities for achievement of goals not related to money and power that could empower personal growth and contribute to sustained happiness.

Since the beginning of the Industrial Revolution, the ability for one person to acquire massive amounts of resources is unprecedented. Left to the devices of the ego, humans will continue to acquire resources far beyond what is actually needed for survival. In fact, we are the only species on the planet that takes more than it needs. The original titans of industry, such as Andrew Carnegie, Henry Ford, J.P. Morgan, and John D. Rockefeller, are early examples of the human ego taking advantage of the Industrial Revolution to acquire great wealth. For these men, risk taking paid off in the extreme. Our competitive instincts and our continuing drive to acquire resources (primarily in the form of money), together with ownership of industrial complexes by individuals, has warped our modern society to extremes of wealth and poverty.

Another aspect of the human mind is that we tend to not see external circumstances as contributing to our level of success and self-esteem. People who come from a background of wealth and privilege will tend to attribute their success to their own efforts and will not see their success as being based on their initial position in life, privileged race/gender, or ongoing financial opportunities. Our brains relate the presence of power and resources to our own abilities rather than support from others. From the ego's perspective, people who do not have an equal position in life are judged to be intrinsically inferior.

The opposite is true of people born into a disadvantaged life with limited opportunities. They often do not realize it is just their circumstances making life more difficult. They may compare themselves to more privileged people and judge themselves to be inadequate. They tend to have low self-esteem and feel hopeless. People with low self-esteem have higher rates of anxiety, loneliness, and depression. Low self-esteem can cause problems with friendships and romantic relationships, seriously impair academic and job performance, and lead to increased vulnerability to drug and alcohol abuse.

The ego's lack of compassion for those in disadvantaged circumstances, combined with the extremes of wealth and poverty brought on by the Industrial Revolution, contributes to many of the imbalanced political, economic, and societal structures in place today. The egos of the wealthy and privileged seek to maintain their wealth and power at the expense of those of disadvantaged socioeconomic class, nationality, race, or gender.

The Collective Ego

The concept of a collective ego is one that explains collective human behavior in many situations. In our evolutionary past, defense of the tribe and suspicion of other tribes were a necessity for group survival. Allegiance to the tribe and competition with other tribes was part of everyday life. Many of the principles and purposes of the ego play out at a group and an individual level. For example, behavior generated by the collective ego plays out today in the rather innocuous system of sports teams from various cities competing with each other. Fanatical support for the home team and disdain for the opposing team is a common occurrence. This trait traces back to our evolutionary tribal history.

However, there is a darker side to the collective ego. Today, it is countries rather than tribes that play out the geopolitical competition that can escalate to war and much destruction of life and property. A charismatic, ego-driven leader can tap into the egoic nature of citizens to create collective fear and hatred of enemy countries. The drive for acquisition of resources on the national level can lead to invasion and plundering of weaker countries. Today's weaponry has destructive power far beyond what our ancestors could even imagine. The majority of world leaders possessing these weapons are motivated by an ego-driven lust for power and money.

Hitler's Nazi Germany is the most infamous example of the destructive power of the collective ego. The German sense of superiority over others was the work of the collective ego. The same type of drama is currently playing out on the world stage, often in more subtle ways. Modern demagogues vie for money and power by manipulating their citizens into hating and fearing rival nations, minorities, or religions. It is typically the common people in these competing countries who suffer from their leader's ego-driven behavior. Egoic leaders are often resistant to cooperation with other countries to solve global problems, such as climate change. Nationalism is the modern term used for these collective egoic tendencies on the nation level.

Even beyond these ego-created difficulties, there is a larger question of the purpose of life and what meaning we are to take from our existence on Earth. An existence at the mercy of our egos, driven by the unconscious imperative of survival and reproduction, is quite a dismal thought for many. Simply following the ego's dictates creates a dystopian reality concerned only with fulfillment of unconscious biological goals. Life under the rule of ego alone is lean on happiness and rich in strife. This is because the ego is never satisfied in the present, is self-serving and transactional, and cares little about the well-being of others except for what they offer to our continued survival. The ego dictates a preprogrammed life with little real personal choice, compassion for others, or pursuit of a higher calling.

Is there more to life than simply living out our ego's preprogramming? This is the question we will explore in Chapter 6.

CH6

Our Spirit in a Human Body

We are not human beings having a spiritual experience. We are spiritual beings having a human experience.

Pierre Teilhard de Chardin
1918

For some people, the description of our biological self is sufficient, requiring no further exploration.

They see life as no more than our biological existence in the observed universe. However, young Seth's existential dilemma evoked by the slaying of his rival points to the possibility that there is more to the story—and to the universe. From the ego's perspective, Seth carried out his evolutionary imperative by helping to defeat the rival tribe and procuring the resources deemed necessary for his own tribe's survival. His ego clearly demonstrated evolutionary fitness. His status within the tribe and self-esteem improved, and he experienced a measure of temporary happiness from reaching his egoic goal. There should be no place for sadness or remorse in his moment of glory.

Yet still, when Seth looked into his dying opponent's eyes, he saw more than just a biological organism who was an obstacle to his success. He also saw a reflection of himself and felt the pain of another living being as his life drained out. Even though Seth's opponent was an impediment to his own evolutionary success, he felt a connection with him that transcended Seth's egoic perspective. Seth's mixed feelings were a result of his ego drives conflicting with some unseen bond with his opponent. In this chapter, we begin our exploration of the spiritual aspects of life beyond our biology-based ego.

The Illusion of Separation

About 86 percent of the world's population adhere to some religious belief, and the remaining 14 percent are either atheist or agnostic. A central tenet of most world religions is that of a higher power (God, universal consciousness, supernatural being, etc.) that is in connection with something within each human being (soul, spirit, higher self, essence). Another central tenet is that all human beings share an energetic or spiritual connection such that what impacts one impacts all. As the Buddha said, "When watching after yourself, you watch after others. When watching after others, you watch after yourself." Jesus said, "Love thy neighbor as thyself," and, "The kingdom of God is within you." In these statements, Buddha and Jesus were alluding to the interconnectedness of all human beings with each other and with a higher power. This interconnectedness can be expanded to include all living beings and the universe itself.

We live an existence with competing realities. In one reality, we are spiritual beings, all interconnected, with love and universal consciousness as the ultimate truth. In another reality, we are biological beings doing our best to survive here on Earth. This requires competition for resources and violence for protection. The quandary between these two realities forms much of the human experience.

The ego sees itself as a separate unit in competition with all other living beings. The ego strives to gain at the expense of others. Egoic love and cooperation are only practiced when a personal benefit can result. Many spiritual traditions call this "the illusion of separation," in that the ego blinds us to the unseen web of interconnectedness. The ego does not believe what cannot be perceived by the five senses. This precludes consciousness of not only physical phenomena beyond our senses' level of perception, but also phenomena beyond this plane of physical existence. These phenomena beyond the plane of perceived physical existence are difficult to prove with the scientific method. Therefore, many scientists and other literalists struggle with the idea of any spiritual or energetic phenomena other than what can be sensed and measured. Spiritual seekers are left to rely on teachings from spiritual leaders, as well as their own personal experiences, to determine what lies beyond ego.

Transpersonal Psychology

As we explore the world of spiritual and metaphysical experience, we leave the world of evolutionary psychology and enter the world of transpersonal psychology. Transpersonal psychology, sometimes called spiritual psychology, integrates the spiritual and transcendent aspects of the human experience within the framework of modern psychology. Transpersonal psychology is not meant to be a replacement for evolutionary psychology or psychology in general. Instead, its intention is to honor our egoic experience of the world while exploring what aspects of our experience can transcend ego.

In fact, ignoring our egoic tendencies and assuming we are better than our egos has its own term in the field of transpersonal psychology—*spiritual bypassing*. Spiritual bypassing occurs when we suppress or deny aspects of the ego—such as difficult thoughts, emotions, and memories—and pretend they have no impact on us. The true spiritual seeker acknowledges the ego, recognizes its purpose and usefulness, and then explores the realm of experience beyond our egoic tendencies that can release the ego's grip on our behavior.

In the context of spirituality and religion, the ego often takes on a different meaning than in the world of psychology. Our spirit (soul, higher self, essence) is seen as our true self, while we inhabit our bodies as a vehicle for our human experience. The ego is an illusory self that deludes us into living in fear rather than from love. The higher calling of our spiritual self is toward unconditional love, oneness rather than separation, the interconnection of all living beings, and compassion rather than defensiveness. Our spiritual self does not live in the past or future but is fully present in each moment. Death is not seen as the end to be feared but a new beginning.

From a spiritual perspective, the ego is often seen as an obstacle to living our human life as a fully actualized spiritual being. Therefore, the ego is seen as something to be overcome or avoided in order to lead a true spiritual life. The ego seeks to maintain the illusion of separation and the idea that we must defend ourselves at all costs. As written in *A Course in Miracles,* "It is certainly apparent by now why the ego regards spirit as its 'enemy.' The ego arose from the separation, and its continued existence depends on your continuing belief in the separation."

In some spiritual traditions, as well as in popular culture, the ego appears as a vague ghost, stalking us to induce our worst behaviors. It is not clear just what exactly the ego is. Rather than examine it, we are taught to turn our backs and avoid it as a Christian might avoid the devil. The ego can be seen as the basis for sin, resulting in guilt and shame if we act on the ego's impulses. Our attempts to overcome acting on self-interest and to put the needs of others first by sheer willpower are usually short-lived. Suppression and avoidance of the ego pushes it into the dark corners of our psyche, causing us to act out of our shadow rather than awareness.

The Ego in Eastern Philosophy

In Chapter 3, we explored the true nature of ego with the realization that the ego is just a mental representation of ourselves with no solid foundation in reality. Although we are compelled to protect our sense of self or ego, we know from neurobiology that this self is an illusion. In

Buddhism, the term *anatta* refers to the doctrine of "non-self"—that there is no unchanging, permanent self, soul, or essence in human experience. The concept of anatta asserts that there is no spiritual or higher self, in addition to there being no real psychological self or ego. This is one of the fundamental differences between Hinduism and Buddhism, with the former asserting that *atman* (higher-self, soul) exists. Buddhism is somewhat unique in this respect compared to other world religions.

It is clear from Buddhist teaching that the ego is an illusion and an obstacle to enlightenment—the complete dissolution of one's identity as a separate self. What Buddha determined through self-inquiry thousands of years ago has been confirmed by modern neurobiology and evolutionary psychology. The ego is an image of ourselves fully created by our minds. Our egoic self believes it is an individual human existence and that it must defend itself in the world to survive.

In Eastern spirituality, the state of being trapped in the illusory belief that one is the ego is known as *maya* or *samsara*. The ego is ultimately unaware and unconscious of its own true nature. We must overcome this delusion to see the truth of ourselves and our existence.

The Dalai Lama said, "Selflessness is not a case of something that existed in the past becoming nonexistent. Rather, this sort of 'self' is something that never did exist. What is needed is to identify as nonexistent something that always was nonexistent. This seemingly solid, concrete, independent, self-instituting 'I' under its own power actually does not exist at all." It is not that the ego disappears through enlightenment, but that the belief in the ego's solidarity, the identification with ego's representations, is abandoned in the realization that the ego is an illusion.

Eckhart Tolle comments that "to the extent that the ego is present in an individual, that individual is somewhat insane psychologically," in reference to the ego's nature as compulsively hyperactive and compulsively self-centered. He adds, "The ego is a dysfunctional relationship with the present moment." Unfortunately, living from ego is normal in our society and goes unrecognized as the source of much behavior that could be classified as insane.

Reaching Enlightenment

Religious followers and spiritual seekers often espouse spiritual beliefs in love and eternal life but continue to go about their lives in fear, separation, and frantic avoidance of death. They possess an intellectual understanding of these principles and may feel superior to others because they have found the truth, but they continue to live life from their egoic perspective. These spiritual concepts have not penetrated from mental constructs to a deep knowing.

True realization that we are ultimately spiritual beings having an earthly experience shatters old beliefs and is life altering. Our worldview makes a 180-degree turn away from fear toward love and acceptance. Living this realization results in priorities and behaviors that are quite different from our old life lived in illusion. Others may question our choices and actions when they are no longer motivated by our ego. We live in the world but not of the world.

The term enlightenment, like the term ego, can have several different meanings, depending on context and culture. There are several commonalities of the meaning of enlightenment across various spiritual paths. These commonalities are:

- A sense of unity and connectedness with God, all living beings, the universe, or reality itself

- An intensity of experience that is profound, often with a powerful sense of universal love

- A sense of clarity in which life seems to make sense and the puzzle pieces fall into place

- Surrender to the flow of life, whereby we stop trying to control life or those around us

- A sense that an intangible something—one's beliefs, purpose, and perspective—has permanently changed

The common thread in the above attributes of enlightenment is that the ego is no longer in control of our thoughts and actions. The fearful trance in which we must always be on guard and in control evaporates and we can relax into these universal truths.

In Chapter 3, we touched on the topic of altruism or egoic love that assumes a reciprocal benefit will occur at some later point, versus non-egoic or unconditional love emanating from our enlightened self that truly expects nothing in return. Discerning between the two can be difficult for both the giver and the receiver. In fact, the very same behavior could be categorized as either, depending on the subconscious intention of the giver.

An example of a true act of unconditional love would be a donation or act of service where the recipient does not know the source of the gift, and no one else observes the gift being given. The gift would also need to be given to someone who is not in the same community as the giver so that no vicarious benefit can occur to the giver. In this example, no egoic benefit could come to the giver, and only unconditional love or compassion could be the true motivation.

Of course, an act of unconditional love can occur without these conditions on the gift, but the selfless intention and attitude of the giver would have to be the same as in the example. Such an act would come from a place of universal love and compassion, where the giver believes in the interconnectedness of all living things and that there is no separation between the giver and receiver. Providing an act of love is in itself a reward, as it is an expression of open-heartedness. Honestly applying the test outlined in the example to our acts of love will likely show that true unconditional love emanating from an enlightened perspective is a rare thing.

Enlightenment and the Brain

Neuroscientists, such as Andrew Newberg, M.D., have conducted extensive research on changes in the brains of enlightened individuals from various spiritual backgrounds. Activity in the brain is examined with functional magnetic resonance imaging (fMRI). These machines can track moment-to-moment processes and changes in brain activity when a person performs tasks or engages in spiritual practices. While these studies cannot reveal the whole of the enlightenment experience, they do show that enlightenment entails shifts in brain patterns that include reduced activity in brain centers associated with ego functioning.

The fMRI scans show that enlightenment appears to involve a decrease in activity in the *frontal lobe* of the neocortex, which corresponds to a reduction in reasoning and abstract thought. There is also a decrease in activity in the *parietal lobe* near the top of the neocortex, particularly when subjects report an intense sense of unity with the world. The usual function of the parietal lobe is to take all the sensory information coming into the brain and create our sense of self—and to establish our relationship to the outer world. A reduction in parietal lobe activity coincides with a dissolution of the sense of a separate self and a blurring of the delineation between self and the rest of the world.

These brain scans of spiritual practitioners also revealed changes in the *thalamus*, a central structure of the limbic brain that receives sensory input and helps us build reality models of the world. A reduction in activity of the *amygdala*, the brain's fearful watchdog, is also associated with enlightenment. All of these brain regions are involved in ego functions and in maintaining the sense of a fearful, separate self. The fact that enlightenment reduces activity in these regions is confirmation that the ego is merely a set of brain functions that facilitate survival and is not a true self.

The Puzzle of Life on Earth

As discussed previously, most of the world's religions adhere to the belief that there is a God or higher power and that we all carry a spiritual essence within us. However, the concept of a separate spirit or soul within each of us is somewhat counter to the idea of oneness and the illusion of separation. This seeming contradiction can be resolved through the analogy of an interconnected network or matrix wherein all are a part of the whole and what impacts one impacts all. A related analogy is that of a diamond, where each facet represents a spiritual self that cannot be separated from the whole of the diamond. The whole of the diamond can be seen as God, or universal consciousness, from which we are not separate.

This brings us to one of the central puzzles of life on Earth. If separation is an illusion and we are all interconnected souls, why on earth do we possess egos that promote the opposite view of survival of the fittest and competition with our fellow humans? Why do we find ourselves in a situation where our ego's drive for preservation of our physical body puts us in conflict with the loving, fearless nature of our spiritual self? Our spiritual selves and egoic selves seem to be direct polar opposites, at cross purposes with each other. This quandary is not only true on Earth, but would be true of any life form in our universe where living organisms must ingest each other to survive and there is competition for limited resources. I believe no human can provide a definitive answer to this question, and it is best left as a koan for each of us to ponder.

In *Conversations with God,* author Neal Donald Walsch points to one possible explanation for this quandary. "Before creation, there was only That-Which-Is, which cannot know or experience itself fully, without something it is not. It cannot know itself as love, since nothing exists but love. It cannot know itself as giving, since nothing else exists to give to. It cannot experience itself in myriad ways because everything is one." Our present creation then, in Walsch's viewpoint, is established by and within God, so that sentience can exist which does not directly remember its true nature as God. Split into infinite forms, all life can live, experience, and recreate its nature as God, rather than just "know" itself as the creator in theory. Following this logic, ego, physical separation, and competition are needed to split God into myriad facets so that each of us can explore our nature as a separate self.

Walsch's concept of God exploring various facets of Herself can be applied on the individual level as well. The conflict between our selfish ego drives and our spiritual quest for universal love and unity creates a tension that allow us to explore aspects of ourselves and know ourselves more fully. Sorting out our ego-motivated behavior required for earthly existence versus the expression of our higher self toward spiritual attainment is a unique type of adversity that demands the attention of the spiritual seeker.

Both psychologists and spiritual teachers often point to the role adversity plays in personal and spiritual growth. Adversity in our lives points out our weaknesses, unhealed wounds, and maladaptive behaviors. At the same time, adversity provides an opportunity to challenge our fears, build our capacity to heal, and make changes in our approach that lead to more peaceful, happier lives.

When adversity is avoided or kept from us, it prevents the seeds of character, learning, resilience, creativity, and conviction from germinating. It is the learning that comes from adversity that creates the opportunity for growth. We can move forward on the path to enlightenment when we shift our perception to see adversity as an opportunity for growth and not as a threat to our well-being. Realizing that the egoic separation is an illusion and that our egoic self is merely an artifact of life in physical existence is a pathway back to oneness with God.

Obviously, there is no way to prove or disprove these assertions. Each of us needs to explore what feels true for us. However, it is difficult to deny that Seth's dilemma of egoic achievement and its conflict with some greater sense of connection and oneness with all living beings reside within all of us. If our identification with ego is strong enough and ego is dense enough, we might find it difficult to find the flicker of spirit and connection with universal consciousness within us. In fact, most people live their entire lives from egoic drives, even if they are part of some organized religion.

Even in these cases, the dissatisfaction with ego and the yearning for something greater than ourselves is present. We seem to know intuitively that there is another path beyond being a slave to the ego's desires. Just what this yearning is and how to pursue it remains a mystery to most. Religion is, in large part, humanities' attempt to make sense of this quandary. However, if the ego coopts the process, religion becomes a spiritual dead-end. Transcendent religion escapes the illusions that egoic religion perpetuates. This is the highest purpose of religion, to support our quest to move beyond ego and find peace in the realm of spirit.

The reason (if there is one) for the predicament we humans find ourselves in of conflicting impulses toward separation and competition versus universal love and unity may never be known definitively. However, here we are, living out this drama on a day-to-day basis as best we can. Our aspiration then is to become conscious of the drama these conflicting roles create in our daily lives.

This awareness holds the promise of taming the wild horse. The ego is not some mysterious enemy to be feared; it is a phenomenon to be understood for its purpose as well as its limitations. Putting the ego in context allows us to create some space between our higher self and our troublesome thoughts and emotions. This path of consciousness and containment of our ego for the promotion of our general happiness and compassion for others will be explored further in Chapter 7.

CH7

The Ego
Owner's Manual

Row, row, row your boat
gently down the stream,
merrily, merrily, merrily,
merrily, life is but a dream.

Eliphalet Oram Lyte
1881

Transcendence of ego as the path
to enlightenment is the stated goal
of many spiritual traditions, particularly
in east Asian religions.

While this is a noble goal, teachings on how to accomplish this are typically short on specifics of just what we are transcending and how to go about it. Understanding the biological basis for ego that has been established in previous chapters creates an opportunity to take a more specific and knowledgeable approach to managing our ego and provides a foundation to explore what lies beyond. In this chapter, steps to support the journey based on our new understanding of the nature of ego are presented. We will explore alternatives to unconsciously following our egoic drives.

Appreciating the ego's purpose and limitations allows us to put the ego in perspective and observe its functioning consciously. Through mindfulness of our ego, we can develop a practice of noticing when our egoic tendencies are controlling our behavior—a key to shifting control from ego to higher self. Learning approaches to embrace our higher self provides freedom from the directives of ego.

In some cases, enlightenment can happen spontaneously and instantaneously. But for most of us, managing our ego and operating from our spiritual essence is a slow unfolding, with both insights and setbacks marking the path. Our trust in ego is highly ingrained from childbirth throughout life, and with good reason. Our trust in ego is what has allowed us to survive to this point. However, our ego has programmed us to survive, not thrive. Learning to trust in our higher self (spirit, essence, presence of God) and let go of attachment to ego is the path to truly leading a peaceful life. Typically, this is a slow process, just as development of ego attachment was a slow process. Self-compassion and self-patience are necessary to allow the process to evolve naturally.

This shifting in trust from the illusions perpetuated by ego to the enlightened perspective is a process of challenging long-held beliefs about ourselves and the world, and breaking through to realization of truth about our existence. An example of this change in perception is moving from seeing ourselves as separate and different from other living beings to the ability to see ourselves as interconnected with all of life and the unified field of consciousness. Such a shift starts with an intellectual understanding, then becomes ingrained in our being after repeatedly challenging our thoughts to see existence from a higher perspective. Some practical steps to living in harmony with our ego while transitioning trust from ego to spirit are described below.

Understanding How Ego Serves Us

First things first in understanding our ego: We can never let go of ego completely while we are in these human bodies. Some aspects of the ego are necessary to keep us safe and functioning for day-to-day living. The drive to acquire the basic necessities of food, clothing, and shelter is quite necessary to complete our journey here on Earth. Our goal then is not to dispose of our ego. Our goal is to recognize how ego serves us and embrace the necessary aspects of ego while building awareness and releasing the excessive and destructive aspects of ego that do not serve us.

Our ego provides the sense of "I" necessary for us to navigate and function in the world. We could not complete school, hold a steady job, or raise a family without our ego. The ego sets boundaries with others to help keep us safe, both physically and emotionally. The ego motivates us to reach goals that are important to our well-being. It is necessary equipment on this planet.

A first step on the path is to fully understand and accept our ego for how it serves us—and to release the guilt and shame related to having an ego. With all the various meanings and emotions attached to the word ego, we must repeatedly come back to the truth that our ego is just our biological survival mechanism for our time on Earth. It is not good or bad, right or wrong. It just is. The ego comes standard with the human body. It is how we evolved to maintain the human species. This view of the ego is a revolutionary idea for most, and the connotations will take some time to absorb.

As the spiritual teacher Adyashanti states, "Ego is neither positive nor negative. Those are simply concepts that create more boundaries. Ego is just ego, and the disaster of it all is that you, as a spiritual seeker, have been conditioned to think of the ego as bad, as an enemy, as something to be destroyed. This simply strengthens the ego. In fact, such conclusions arise from the ego itself. Pay no attention to them. Don't go to war with yourself; simply inquire into who you are."

For most of us, the belief that the ego is a bad thing is deeply embedded in our psyche. Even if the term ego is not used, cultural and religious values that condemn our egoic tendencies are widespread. In Western culture many aspects of ego, particularly the selfish and aggressive aspects, are judged to be bad or wrong in children who then grow up to feel guilt and shame about these traits in themselves. Christianity espouses the concept of sin, which is assigned to many behaviors that are simply born out of ego functions. "Thou shalt not..." translates to thou shalt not have an ego. Our attempt to suppress culturally condemned aspects of our ego in order to be socially acceptable is not a sustainable solution. Pushing unsavory aspects of ego into the shadows of our subconscious takes them out of our conscious control. Such aspects will find a way to express, often in passive-aggressive and destructive ways.

Therefore, we must appreciate our ego for how it serves us and for how it is trying to protect us. We would not condemn a friend who works day and night to keep our bodies safe and fed, and neither should we condemn our ego for doing the same. The ego needs to be befriended and understood for what it is attempting to provide, which is survival and reproduction. There is no need or benefit in criticizing and condemning our ego. The ego provides an essential function. Criticizing our ego is like criticizing our heart or lungs for doing their jobs. That would make no sense. By shifting our perspective to be accepting and grateful of ego rather than condemning it, we begin to put our ego in context and create some space for our higher self to thrive.

Some may fear that if we do not shame and suppress our ego, it will run amok and cause damage to those around us. This punitive approach to managing ego is born out of our ideas of a judgmental and vindictive God and our internalized disciplinary parent. It is a "command and control" approach to keeping our ego in check that depends on the illusion of fear and separation to achieve its ends. Ironically, it is our ego trying to control our ego. This approach perpetuates the feelings of fear and shame related to ego.

A more enlightened approach is to return to the truth of who we are—loving spiritual beings, interconnected with each other and all of life. Why would we want to harm another when in doing so we harm ourselves? We can observe our ego's tendencies without allowing them to dictate our behavior. We can learn to act from our authentic higher self. No fear, guilt, or shame is needed to motivate us to act in loving, compassionate, and considerate ways. We allow ourselves to be free and, in doing so, create freedom for all.

The Role of Psychology

Nearly all Western psychology deals with improving the ego by changing thought patterns that lead to painful emotions. Western psychology assumes the ego is all that we are, and our only hope is to get the ego to function as best we can. Psychology addresses problems in our developmental history to determine which are negatively impacting us and attempts to resolve these problems so they no longer affect our present-day functioning. While this ego improvement model is a limited view, psychology still plays an important role in personal growth and preparation for transcendence.

Psychological/ego issues from the past generally fall into two categories. The first category is neglect: the lack of positive influences that should have happened but didn't, such as reliable nurturing from a parent. The second category is abuse: the presence of damaging experiences that should not have happened but did, such as physical or emotional trauma. Healing the first category typically requires that we pursue missing experiences to fill the voids in our development. Healing the second category usually requires some type of trauma release work. Whether through psycho-therapy, self-help books, group experiences, or healing relationships, effectively dealing with such issues facilitates the ability to live in the present moment.

Transcendent experiences can and do occur in spite of unhealed wounds from the past. However, such experiences are usually part of what is termed non-abiding awakening. We can temporarily awaken to our true nature but get pulled back into our egoic nature by life events that trigger our unhealed wounds. An example of this is a critical comment from a partner that reminds us of a critical parent. If we have not dealt with parental wounding, the pain from the past will return and our ego will immediately take charge in an attempt to defend our sense of self. Any enlightened state is lost in the egoic reaction. We then must intervene in the egoic thought-emotion cycle to regain our composure and perspective to see the situation from our true nature once again. Most of us will experience this cycle quite often on the path to enlightenment. The more unattended psychological wounds we carry, the more often we will get triggered into an egoic reaction and find ourselves out of an enlightened state. Therefore, psychological work is an important step on the path of transcendence.

An honest inventory of egoic wounding and missing experiences from our past to see where more psychological work is needed is a necessary step on our path. As an example, an insecure attachment style from inadequate parenting is an ego development issue that, until it is dealt with, will repeatedly return to interfere with adult relationships and keep us from consistently maintaining an open heart.

We all tend to have a particular complex of thoughts and feelings we return to repeatedly that feels like "us." As discussed in Chapter 4, an egoic cycle often develops where a thought generates an emotion, which then generates more defensive thoughts. Repeating a certain pattern of thoughts and emotions leads to developing this particular sense of us. This complex is our personal style of ego, assembled from our genetic propensities and childhood experiences. Development of this conditioned egoic complex typically starts with repeated childhood experiences that generate neural pathways between the neocortex and limbic brain in a particular pattern. This "us" can be miserable or relatively happy, depending on the complex that developed. Our particular complex becomes our set point that we return to because it is so familiar.

For an example of such an egoic complex, let's consider an infant whose single mother has a hectic job with constantly changing work hours. As the child develops, the mother is inconsistently available to be with the child. Mom often does not come home when she says she will. As this pattern repeats, the child will begin to relate the feelings of abandonment, sadness, and disappointment with the thoughts that she cannot trust people and that she is not important. The brain synapse related to these thoughts and feelings will begin to fire and wire together. After some time, this state of being mistrustful and disappointed becomes so familiar that it becomes the core of the child's ego. All future experiences will be viewed through this lens.

Our particular egoic complex is likely both our most unconscious pattern of behavior and the most difficult aspect of the ego to release. We are highly attached to this complex and unaware of this attachment. The egoic complex is a rut we fall back into with the slightest provocation. Even if this egoic complex is continuously painful, the bond to the complex is typically stronger than the aversion to the pain. We will seek out confirmation in our experiences that the world is untrustworthy, dangerous, deceptive, unloving, or whatever other belief that has become part of the egoic complex. This phenomenon is termed *confirmation bias*. We see what we expect to see. Our myopic perception becomes proof that our ego was right all along. We are caught in an illusion of our own making.

The first step in seeing through this illusion is to become aware of it and how it developed. This requires us to jump outside of our typical self-image to see ourselves from a new perspective. We must become the objective observer of ourselves and our history. What is your core wound? What are your strongest ego attachments? In what area does your ego seem to be most defensive? What is your go-to thought/emotion complex? How did it develop? What external stimuli trigger your egoic complex?

Answers to these and similar questions help us to understand our egoic complex and point us toward the wounds and trigger points that ask for our attention in order to work through and release them. Support from others, such as a psychotherapist, is often needed to explore and release these conditioned patterns so we can create true change.

The typical spiritual journeyer will be dealing with both egoic wounding and transcendent spiritual experiences throughout life. We don't need to perfect our ego before we can develop spiritually. Psychological and spiritual work go on concurrently and often are interrelated. We must be open and aware of what life brings us without preconceived notions of how the path should unfold—and respond appropriately.

A tendency to avoid addressing painful egoic wounds in favor of spiritual ideas and practices is spiritual bypassing, which will lead to a spiritual dead end. Suppressing our psychological wounds out of shame or fear of them, or pretending we have evolved beyond them will create a shadow self of these repressed aspects of ego. This shadow self creates suffering for us and those around us through unconscious acting out. Finding a balance between psychological and spiritual work, and trusting that the universe is providing the experiences needed to propel us on the path to healing and transcendence, are hallmarks of a maturing spiritual seeker.

Building Ego Awareness

Building awareness of our internal experience is often a prescribed practice on the spiritual path. Developing awareness of when and how our ego is impacting us is a major step in releasing the ego's hold on us. The idea is to bring unconscious thoughts, emotions, beliefs, and patterns into consciousness to observe their often-erroneous nature and provide the opportunity for change.

Chapter 4 included a table that lists aspects of egoic functioning and their evolutionary purpose. Those ego attributes are shown again in Table 3 (pages 65-68), with the inclusion of a transcendent idea for each. The attributes shown in the table all have had a valid purpose in promoting our evolutionary fitness. However, often these functions are maladaptive to the goals of the modern spiritual seeker. When we notice our mind engaging in one of the ego attributes shown, we can challenge the necessity of acting on ego and turn toward the transcendent idea as an alternative perspective to consider. The egoic thought, emotion, or egoic complex of thoughts and emotions can be released in favor of the spiritually based alternative.

Developing the power of self-observation facilitates awareness of our egoic patterns by creating space between our observing higher self and our unconscious ego. Noticing uncomfortable emotions or body sensations can be the signal that the ego is likely at work. Engaging our mind to identify the source thoughts or beliefs underlying the egoic reaction opens the door to alternative thoughts that are in alignment with the truth of who we are as peaceful, loving spiritual beings. This process of observing our ego and shifting focus to the corresponding transcendent idea can happen many times per day. Our egoic patterns of thoughts and emotions are deeply embedded and long-standing, and a concerted and sustained effort is usually required to release the pattern and embrace the truth.

We all have various internal voices that represent our different points of view. These voices are often at odds with each other, resulting in internal conflict and stress. The internal voice of ego is often in conflict with the voice of our higher self. With some practice, we can learn to recognize self-talk emanating from our ego versus that of our higher self. The enlightened internal voice is characterized by a sense of expansion, creativity, and excitement for the possibilities that life holds. Our egoic voice is characterized by a fearful outlook combined with a self-critical tone.

We may have internal arguments in which an optimistic and ambitious idea from our higher self is immediately shot down by the voice of ego: "You are not capable of that." "That's too risky." "What's in it for me?" These are a few examples of the voice of ego pushing back against our enlightened self. Listening to the voice of ego can cause us to lose confidence and play small. When we recognize the voice of ego, it's helpful to remember that our ego's purpose is simply to help us physically survive. The ego has no interest in the infinite possibilities of our higher self. We can thank our ego for keeping us safe and then put our creative energy into our enlightened ideas that fulfill our higher purpose.

Working with Fear

Fear seems to be a constant companion in our lives and is often our most troublesome emotion. Fear is the main tool our ego used to keep our human bodies alive and functioning in our evolutionary past by avoiding dangerous situations and by staying in good standing with the social order. Fear creates a bias toward risk aversion and maintaining the status quo. In the hunter-gatherer communities where our egos evolved, physical threats to our existence were prevalent and fear played an important role. In our modern world, physical threats are less frequent, and fear is often maladaptive in supporting our happiness and fulfillment. Even so, our limbic brain has not evolved since our hunter-gatherer days and will generate a fear response anytime a situation appears to be threatening or we contemplate taking a risk.

Want to ask someone out on a date? The ego's fear of social rejection and lowered self-esteem will make you think twice about it. Want to start that new business? The ego's resistance to upsetting the status quo and the potential money/resource loss can cause you to abandon those plans. Even though there is no actual risk of death in these endeavors, the ego acts as if there is. We instinctively think of the worst-case scenario and make decisions based on it.

To counter our ego's fearful tendencies, we can start by remembering our ego's automatic reactions are largely irrelevant in modern society. Though we seldom realize it, avoidance of death is at the root of our fear. Our limbic brain puts a life-or-death emotional spin on relatively benign situations. Our ego sees threats where there are none. The acronym FEAR—False Evidence Appearing Real—has gained some popularity as a reminder of this illusion.

We can notice our emotional reactions to a given situation but pause and avoid taking immediate action out of fear. Engage the logical neocortex to second-guess the knee-jerk reactions of the limbic brain. Besides the worst-case outcome, think of the best-case outcome and then the most realistic outcome. Base your actions on the realistic scenario. Often even in the worst-case scenario, the outcome is not as bad as we imagine it. The potential benefits of taking the risk often far outweigh the potential downside.

From the spiritual viewpoint, we can shift our thinking from the egoic perspective to the transcendent perspective. Remember, our human bodies are temporary vehicles for our existence on Earth. Death of our bodies is not the end of our eternal spiritual essence. Our ego is not aware that life transcends death and therefore defends our human body at all costs. Our higher self knows the truth and has no fear of the decay and death of the body. Embracing this truth allows us to take risks and reach for our full potential without the constant interruption of our ego's fearful voice.

Meditation

Meditation is a mainstay of self-awareness practices and can be quite useful in addressing the ego. Meditation provides focused time to observe our egoic patterns and move beyond them.

Vipassana meditation, sometimes called insight meditation, in particular is quite useful for building ego awareness. The word Vipassana means to see things as they really are. Rather than focusing on just one aspect of our experience, such as breathing, Vipassana meditation seeks to bring all our experience into awareness, including thoughts, mental images, emotions, and body sensations.

Vipassana meditation can be used to identify and track one aspect of experience or all of our experience in aggregate. Meditation can be tailored to observe particular aspects of the ego. For example, we can decide to use a meditation session to specifically notice the emotion of fear and the thoughts that precede the fear. Repeated meditation on different aspects of ego is one of the best ways to uncover our conditioned egoic complex. Once the complex comes into awareness, we can practice shifting focus to an alternative transcendent idea. Meditators are encouraged to develop your own transcendent idea that applies to your particular egoic complex. (Guided meditations to promote ego awareness and the transcendent ideas are listed in the Appendix.)

Table 3 – Ego Attributes and Their Spiritual Alternatives

EGO ATTRIBUTE	EVOLUTIONARY PURPOSE	TRANSCENDENT IDEA
Fear	Alerts to danger and primes the body to take action. Blood supply to the muscles is increased and the mind becomes focused on fighting or finding escape routes. Fear in the form of risk aversion promotes survival by minimizing exposure to dangerous situations. Fears that seem unreasonable and disproportionate are called phobias, which may represent inherited hardwired tendencies to fear certain objects or organisms.	Fear protects our physical bodies but has no meaning to our spirit, which is eternal and therefore does not fear death. Our ego believes we can be hurt and die but is unaware of our eternal spiritual essence that knows only love. Remember the truth of who you are. Our bodies are only our vehicle for human experience and will decay and die. Our true essence lives on forever, outside of time and space.
Anger	A protection of perceived mental or physical boundaries. Can provoke violence. Acts of retribution signal to another the cost of provoking anger in this and future situations. Anger may therefore be costly to the actor in the short run but, in the long run, it may be adaptive in modifying future behavior of others.	Nothing real can be threatened, so what are we really protecting? We are projecting our fears onto another then reacting defensively toward our self-created threat. See through this illusion. When anger arises, thank it for its effort to protect your body and give it permission to let go. Channel anger toward social injustice into loving action.

EGO ATTRIBUTE	EVOLUTIONARY PURPOSE	TRANSCENDENT IDEA
Sadness	Weakens our motivation to continue the present course of action. May be a means of telling the person to stop current strategies and conserve resources since they are unrewarding. A sign of lowered self-esteem. Could also be a signal that help is required.	Allow emotions to flow through and release. Sadness is a natural part of human life. If sadness is chronic, examine which beliefs you are attached to that create continuous disappointment. How does sadness feel comfortable and familiar? Seek help when needed.
Jealousy	Forces us to be alert to signs of deception by partners. May activate aggressive behaviors to force the defecting partner back to original relationship or deter partner and trespassing partner from continuing in the new relationship.	Jealousy is the mistaken belief that love is a limited commodity. We believe love comes from special relationships and can only come from the people we designate. Release control of sources of love and practice unconditional love to all that cross your path.
Love	Love for family members increases co-operation and altruism to promote fitness of family unit. Passionate love in mating can further reproductive goals by cementing the pair bond long enough to produce and raise children.	Practice unconditional love that is detached from the reciprocal benefit of your actions. Shift perception from the illusion of separation to realization of oneness. Love for others is love for self. Use personal relationships to practice release of egoic love and to tap into universal love.
Happiness	Provides emotional reward for achieving desired goals that contribute to reproductive fitness. Happiness results from obtaining resources, mates, children, or raised social status. Happiness is a temporary state followed by discontentment to motivate achievement of additional goals.	Release pursuit of happiness in favor of pursuit of truth. Egoic happiness is a fleeting reward, but surrender into presence and acceptance of what is creates sustainable peacefulness that is independent of life circumstances. Put trust in spirit, not ego.
Disgust	Disgust initiates avoidance of potentially dangerous people or situations. Disgust is also the fear of ingesting an undesirable substance. Sexual disgust with family serves to inhibit inbreeding.	Allow your higher self to guide you to safety and support. Respond with love, not react out of fear. Use love and compassion to facilitate change.
Guilt	Remorseful feeling that follows self-awareness of having been unfair to family or tribal members. May serve to drive more cooperative or generous behavior in future encounters to promote reciprocal cooperative behavior.	Practice self-forgiveness by seeing your past from a new perspective. Release your belief in sin. Treat your past self with kindness and understanding. See through the veil that inhibits love for self and others.

EGO ATTRIBUTE	EVOLUTIONARY PURPOSE	TRANSCENDENT IDEA
Anxiety	Anxiety is a combination of fear and desire. Provides motivation to avoid an undesired outcome and to pursue a desired outcome.	Put trust in spirit to create the highest and best outcome for all involved. Release the belief that ego knows best. Embrace the not knowing and release the need to control the future.
Self-esteem	Provides a self-measure of fitness for survival and reproduction. Low self-esteem is subconsciously linked to potential death, either physical or genetic, and is therefore highly anxiety provoking.	Our ego believes we are not good enough and must always try harder. Our spirit exists beyond judgment and knows that anything other than love is an illusion.
Defensiveness	Mitigates fear and anxiety resulting from perceived threats to survival fitness (self-esteem) by providing rationalizations against failure and outside negative judgments.	No defense is required because there is nothing real to defend. The ego believes it is real and must be defended, but it is just a mental construct. Your spiritual essence cannot be harmed.
Competitive-ness	Promotes success against competitors for acquisition of resources, mates, or social status. Wining temporarily raises self-esteem.	Ego mistakenly believes in the polarities of win/lose, good/bad, right/wrong, better than/less than. Spirit does not know separation, duality, or fear of losing.
Greed	Driving force for acquisition of money and resources, sometimes beyond what is needed for survival and attraction of suitable mates.	Ego believes we are separate and always lacking. Trust in spirit rather than ego to provide your needs.
Thoughts	Thoughts about the present help us evaluate the most effective action in each situation. Thoughts about the past or future provide the ability to learn from past experience and plan for success in the future. Thoughts may be distorted by limited sensory perception and cognitive dissonance.	We are not our thoughts and our thoughts are not the same as reality. Our mind generates thoughts based on limited perception and past experiences. We create our own reality with our thoughts by believing and acting on them.
Negativity Bias	Propensity to think of and act on the worst-case scenario in any situation. Promotes survival by biasing awareness and action toward potential danger.	Remember our spiritual essence cannot be threatened and cannot die. See through the egoic veil in yourself and others with love and compassion. Pursue the best and highest good for all involved.

EGO ATTRIBUTE	EVOLUTIONARY PURPOSE	TRANSCENDENT IDEA
Memories	Short-term and long-term memory serve to store relevant information for later recall in the service of dealing with dangerous situations, creating social bonds, acquiring resources, mating, and child rearing. Brain plasticity in youth adapts to the local environment for optimum fitness.	Memories are a distorted record of the past. Notice what beliefs you have developed based on past experiences and memories. Are these egoic beliefs really true? How are they serving you? What does your spiritual essence know is true?
Need to Control	Controlling thoughts and behaviors are an attempt to exert power over others in order to manipulate them to act in a way that is beneficial to the controller. A sense of control can also temporarily mitigate fear and serve as an ego defense.	Our belief in separation and competition causes us to control others. Trust in spirit to guide you, and release fear of the future. Practice loving kindness by allowing others the freedom to make choices as they desire.
Need to be Right	Self-judgments that we are right, and convincing others we are right, raises self-esteem and perceived social status. Being proven wrong lowers self-esteem.	Prioritize love and forgiveness over the need to be right. Realize being right or wrong is a mental construct and does not prove superiority over anyone. It only serves to create separation.

Dissolve into Presence

The discussion to this point has focused on shifting thoughts and emotions away from our egoic tendencies and toward transcendent ideas that reflect the truth of our spiritual essence. Because humans are thinking and feeling beings, the effort to shift our internal experience away from illusion and toward truth is essential. However, a realm of experience exists beyond all thoughts and emotions, beliefs and contracted patterns. This is the transcendent realm of pure presence. Presence occurs when our attachment to ego dissolves and we experience existence from our spiritual essence. Peacefulness permeates our being without a connection to cause. Our sense of self at the center of a finite world disappears, and we are at once everywhere and nowhere. Falling into presence sometimes happens in meditation when we are able to release our repetitive thoughts and emotions without a need to fill the vacuum. We are hyper aware without the need to define the experience with thought.

As discussed earlier, this state of presence can be abiding or non-abiding, depending on our susceptibility to egoic thoughts, emotions, and memories wrestling control away from our peaceful state of stillness. However, once we experience this state of presence in our conscious awareness, we will never forget that it is possible. Our perception of the world permanently shifts, even when we are caught in egoic turmoil. Our higher self is aware that we are battling an illusion.

We all experience fleeting moments of presence that typically go unnoticed. Often at the end of the out-breath and before the in-breath, there is a split second where the mind goes blank. When we are absorbed in an experience that engages all of our senses, such as whitewater rafting, walking in a dense green forest, viewing a rainbow, or making love, the power of the sensory experience can distract us from our typical repetitive thoughts and emotions for a few moments. Becoming aware of these brief experiences of presence can serve as a starting point to understand the nature of a transcendent state of being. Continued spiritual growth is a matter of expanding the frequency and duration of this state of presence.

The transitions from presence to non-presence can actually be a fruitful area of inquiry if we can stay aware of the forces pulling us out of presence. There is typically an egoic pattern of thoughts and emotions that trips us up and takes us out of the state of stillness. For example, if we have the belief that we must stay busy and productive at all times and the fear of being lazy enters our mind while sitting in presence, this complex of fear and thought will resist the state of presence and tug us back into an egoic state. Noticing that such a pattern is our downfall allows us to confront and examine the underlying belief.

Imagine Orville and Wilbur Wright developing the first airplane. Each failed test flight provided information on what was inhibiting flight, allowing for modifications to be made in the design. Once the design was sufficiently improved, their airplane was able to escape the bounds of gravity and soar through the air. In the same respect, we can become aware of our ego traps and develop alternative transcendent ideas that allow us to escape the gravitational pull of our ego.

Releasing Mental Addictions

When we think of addictions, we usually think of an alcoholic or drug addict struggling with a chemical dependency. However, just as drug addicts are attempting to escape the emotional pain they are experiencing, nearly all of us have our mental addictions that provide an escape from experiencing the present moment. Our ego is quite resistant to living in presence because doing so has no evolutionary purpose, and it struggles to maintain the illusion of a separate existence when our egoic machinery is not spinning. When we do manage to escape the ego's hold for a moment of presence, we typically have neglected and suppressed painful emotions that arise, giving us another reason to avoid the present moment. Even though such painful emotions will pass through and dissipate if given the opportunity, we resist the transitory pain entailed and work diligently to avoid the present.

Our mental addictions can take many forms, most of which are deemed socially acceptable but which, in reality, keep us locked in the ego's grip. Obsessive thought itself is a form of addiction. When we grow tired of the suffering created by our own thoughts, we will outsource the mental drama to external stimuli. Modern inventions such as the smartphone are a boon to the ego's purposes. We can escape our internal experience and stay preoccupied with the drama of the outside world for hours on end. Television is another frequent mental addiction and is often nothing more than a babysitter for our minds. In Western culture, workaholism is rampant, motivated by our egoic drive to obtain money and possessions, social admiration from workaholism that raises our self-esteem, and the focus on an outside activity that allows us to escape the present moment. Each of us needs to become aware of our personal addictions so they can be dealt with appropriately.

Dealing with mental addictions starts with the same practice as described above of developing awareness of the patterns we are engaged in. Notice what activity you turn to when the present moment is agitating. Observing our ego feeling uncomfortable with the present moment and inducing us to turn on the news as an escape is an example of such awareness. Once we are aware, we can make the choice to drop our attachment to the mental addiction and move into presence with a willingness to experience whatever the present moment has to offer.

Surrender to Spiritual Guidance

If we could all live as a monk in a monastery, insulated from the ego-driven culture with a guarantee of all of our physical needs being met, living in presence would be a much easier endeavor. But most of us deal directly with modern society, with only ourselves to depend on for our survival. Our unconscious egoic drive for survival and reproduction uses fear of the future as its main tool to motivate us to plan and work for future success. This fear engages our minds in developing endless scenarios about what actions we should take and how our future might play out. This rumination about the future is another major obstacle to living in the present moment.

Planning and acting out of fear from the perspective of our ego's distortions engages our negativity bias and limits our creative thinking of what may be possible. Our minds are incapable of grasping the vast majority of potential outcomes from our actions anyway. This is easily shown by reviewing how past plans have turned out. How often did your life turn out as planned? Likely not very often.

From a spiritual perspective, we seldom personally know what future experiences will facilitate our learning and growth. Our egoic plans are usually focused on acquiring resources or seeking pleasure. Such goals typically do not consider the well-being of all of humanity and the planet. However, spiritual growth derived from universal consciousness seldom prioritizes these human egoic goals. Ironically, just as the ego puts no value judgment on pain or pleasure in achieving its ends of survival and reproduction, our spiritual growth entails both painful and pleasurable experiences in revealing the truth of our spiritual essence. Painful experiences often break our hearts open to reveal where we have been stuck in illusion and where the path back to love lies.

A balanced approach to dealing with the future incorporates developing goals emanating from our higher self with an attitude of cooperation with the universe to guide the way to the best and highest good for all. Decisions made from our higher self will result in a peaceful rather than fearful feeling. The best and highest good may not be initially revealed to us and likely is not a painless and easy life for us. It is the path that will reveal the truth and propel us on our spiritual journey. Another way to state this approach is to set intentions for our life without an attachment to the outcome. We can use our minds to imagine the greatest outcome of our effort, while releasing the ego's control on events having to turn out the way we planned them. This is the metaphysical meaning of the children's song at the opening of this chapter. Row your boat gently down the stream, in cooperation with the flow of life, and always remember our physical existence on Earth is a dream state. We are all in the process of waking up.

In the next chapter, we investigate how ego plays out in the realm of organized spirituality —religion.

CH8

The Ego in Religion

There is a golden thread that runs through every religion in the world. There is a golden thread that runs through the lives and the teachings to all the prophets, seers, sages, and saviors in the world's history, through the lives of all men of truly great and lasting power.

Ralph Waldo Trine
1897

The extraordinary interplay between ego and spirit is nowhere more apparent than in the territory of religion.

While the very purpose of religion is to commune with our own divine essence and to connect with the sacred in all of life, the ego's fearful and self-serving compulsions often pose an obstacle in this pursuit. Great spiritual visionaries such as Jesus, Buddha, and Lao Tzu largely transcended ego and experienced life from an enlightened perspective of unconditional love, oneness of all living beings, and the realization of eternal life. However, adherents to the religions initiated by these visionaries typically have less success in reaching their teachers' enlightened perspectives.

The ego can co-opt anything for its purposes, and religion is no different. Religion can be both a path to spiritual attainment and a channel for egoic expression. How can religion generate both untold suffering and unconditional love? How can religious principles be used to justify terrorism, and conversely result in acts of unconditional love and justice? In this chapter, we first explore aspects of spiritual/religious practices and beliefs that are based in ego and then the universal truths that both transcend ego and the illusion of separation between religions.

Egoic Religion

Evidence of religion has been found at burial sites and in artwork of early Homo sapiens in the Paleolithic period more than 30,000 years ago. In fact, evidence of religion has even been found at burial sites of Neanderthal hominids from more than 40,000 years ago. The desire for connection and understanding of a force greater than ourselves has been present since conscious beings have walked the planet. This search for a deeper meaning to life can be traced to Seth's dilemma of his ego's selfish drive for survival conflicting with his inner knowing of the connection and unity of all living beings. It is derived from the inner sense, even in the earliest humans, that the death of our bodies is not the end of our spiritual journey.

Religion can be defined as an organized system of spiritual beliefs and practices. Spirituality is usually thought of as an individual experience while religion typically connotes a group experience. Organized groups of any type require some sort of structure and hierarchy. Religions and churches have various types of organizational structures that lead to a hierarchy wherein some individuals have power and authority over others. Money is collected from members to fund the religious organization. Religious leaders have the power to dictate the beliefs and behavior of their congregants. The existence of power and money in religion is the only opening the ego needs to exert control over religious adherents.

If someone is spiritually immature, the ego can overpower the higher self's desire to embody love-based teachings and revert to acting out of fear, selfishness, and greed. The ego's drive to acquire power, money, and status often results in religious leaders distorting the original teachings of the founding spiritual teacher. Rather than leading from a position of love and acceptance, religious leaders often employ fear and guilt as tools to control religious followers and convince them to obey the leaders' directives. Rules of behavior enforced by fear and guilt can become institutionalized in religious texts and traditions. This type of ego-driven religion can be termed "egoic religion" because dogmatic adherence to a particular set of beliefs and judgment of those who do not follow them becomes the focus of religious practice, rather than the universal love and interconnectedness originally intended.

Our ancient genetic desire to be tribal members for protection from outside threats and for creation of social bonds is at play in our drive to be members of a religious organization. There is a strong desire within us to define ourselves, whether it's as an American, a Republican or Democrat, Christian or Muslim, or supporter of our local football team. Egoic religion stems from this psychological need for group identity, protection from unfamiliar external groups, confirmation of one's beliefs, and a need for certainty. We all have a desire to be accepted as part of a tribe to promote survival, security, and social status. Egoic religion stems from the ego's need for certainty and superiority, to know that we possess the truth, and that we are right and others are wrong.

The egos of religious followers get a boost from a strict adherence to religious teachings or belief systems because they feel this makes them good people, superior to others. The self-esteem mechanism is engaged to make members feel better about themselves when they follow these prescribed beliefs and behaviors. The ego's defensive engagement of the polarities of right/wrong and good/evil are used by members to self-evaluate their success in adhering to these prescribed beliefs. Members receive admiration from others when they are seen to be successful in following prescribed beliefs and behaviors. Shame and guilt result if members are judged by themselves or others to fail in meeting these religious standards. A feeling of superiority over others based on religious beliefs and fear/hate of those with different beliefs are examples of the ego acting out in religion. For these believers, the fact that other people have different beliefs is a threat, since it implies the possibility that their own beliefs may not be true. They need to convince people with different beliefs that they are wrong to prove to themselves that they are right.

The conviction in superiority over others' beliefs plays out in both the individual and collective ego of religious members. The collective ego is often engaged in religious groups, resulting in tremendous peer pressure to conform to religious doctrine and prescribed behavior. When the collective ego gains control of a group of believers, their religious beliefs become emotion-driven demands on nonbelievers to conform. Even relatively small differences in beliefs can generate strong emotions and result in violence in some cases. The ego's drive to create separation and judgment of others becomes the driving force in the splintering of religious groups and creates suspicion and condemnation of those not in one's group.

There are about 4,300 religions in the world. There are more than 200 distinct Christian denom-inations in the United States alone. Even with the common basis of the Christian Bible, egoic Christians have found a multitude of reasons to create separation. Each point of separation represents a disagreement over beliefs that church leaders could not resolve. Underlying each splintering is the ego that needs to be right, needs to feel superior, and is fearful of differences. Such splintering and separation are present in all of the world's religions.

For egoic religious people, religion isn't about self-improvement or pursuit of the transcendent. It is about adhering to a set of rigid convictions and following the rules prescribed by religious authorities. It's about defending their beliefs against anyone who questions them, asserting their "truth" over others, and imposing their religious beliefs on non-believers. Increasing the number of adherents to a particular belief system acts to reinforce the sense that they are right. Some religions contend that those who do not follow their prescribed beliefs and behaviors will burn in hell for eternity, effectively using fear to force conformance. Evangelical efforts by rank-and-file members to save others from this horrible fate are earnestly carried out by well-meaning parishioners.

Underlying these egoic impulses is a fundamental anxiety and sense of lack caused by our idea of being separate individuals, different from other people, and separated from the world in general.

This separation generates a sense of being cut off, of being divided, like fragments that were once part of a whole. People also have a sense of vulnerability and insecurity caused by our sense of insignificance in the face of the world. These uncomfortable emotions result in a need to reinforce our ego, our sense of self, and to strengthen our identity. Egoic religions and other similar belief systems help us do this. They are a collective thought/emotion complex, stemming from ancient, deep, universal desires for psychological security.

Egoic religion is dangerous because it encourages an "us-versus-them" group mentality. It encourages people to withdraw empathy and understanding from members of other groups, seeing them as inferior and ignorant. Other groups are seen as faceless amorphous entities rather than as collections of unique individuals, each with their own fervent beliefs. When two such groups face off with their different beliefs clashing, judgment and conflict result. Because dogmatic beliefs are part of their core identity, egoic religious followers defend their beliefs just as they would defend their own lives.

The extreme version of the ego in religion is fundamentalism. Religious fundamentalism dictates adherence to ancient traditions with persistent and fanatical calls for an unwavering return to foundational beliefs. It is an attempt to protect the individual and the community from any potential threat or deviation in matters of doctrine and conduct. Any type of change in beliefs or behavior is seen as an existential threat to the collective ego of the religion. In some cases, violence is justified to maintain this strict adherence and to punish those with differing beliefs. Grotesque acts of terrorism are often carried out in the name of fundamentalist religion. These attacks are reflected in the Global Terrorism Index, which shows that religious differences have become the main motive for terrorist acts.

If we step back and take a holistic view of religious belief, we can see that our particular religious belief system is almost entirely dependent on the specific country and culture in which we are born. For example, a child born into a family in the Americas will likely learn that Christianity is the only one true religion and that one must ask God for forgiveness to avoid being sent to hell and to reside in heaven for eternity. A similar child born in Tibet will likely learn Buddhist philosophy and that they must be reincarnated many times to expiate the karma they accumulated in order to reach enlightenment. In both cases the child follows the prescribed beliefs closely in order to be good and achieve the desired goal. Both may look at the other's beliefs as mistaken and even blasphemous. But their beliefs are simply a result of their geographic location. Until recent history, they would not even know of the other's religion.

How can one be right and one be wrong? How can one be validated and the other condemned? Such judgments stem from an egocentric-geocentric religious viewpoint. There are core truths within all religions. We need only look at the teachings of both Jesus and Buddha to see that universal truths reside in both and that egoic judgments are unnecessary.

The ego pursues separation and focuses on differences between individuals and groups, but even our egos have much more in common than our egos would like us to acknowledge. All of our egos are motivated by the unconscious drive for survival and reproduction, using the toolbox of fear and other emotions to control our behavior. We all care for our family members and those in our tribal circle. We all want to feel loved and protected. Most people will respond to a given conflict with similar ego-based behaviors at the same time that they are judging others as different. The ego of one judges the ego of the other in the same way. Despite our similarities, religion practiced on the level of ego is fraught with suspicion and distrust of religious believers following a different path and competition to convert them to one's righteous belief system.

Transcendent Religion

When religious believers are able to rise above the ego's hold and return to the core meaning of their original founder's teaching, a life of freedom and true union with the Divine is possible. The ego's search for reasons to engage in fear and separation are released, and the universal principles of love, unity, and our spirit that transcend death are embraced. This type of "transcendent religion" reflects the higher attributes of our spiritual nature, such as love, compassion, and inclusion. It fosters a sense of the sacred with an unwavering dedication to the truth.

Transcendent religious figures have carried out some of the most virtuous and courageous acts in history in the name of religion. Great moral reformers and activists such as Martin Luther King Jr., Mahatma Gandhi, and Nelson Mandela were inspired by the principles of their religions. Archbishop Desmond Tutu embodies the Christian principles of compassion and forgiveness to the highest degree and spent his life tirelessly campaigning for justice and against oppression.

Transcendent religion transcends the egoic grip on our thoughts, emotions, and behavior. Transcendent religious people don't feel any animosity toward other religious groups. They are happy to investigate other beliefs and welcome the opportunity to go to different temples and religious services. The focus is on similarities and inclusion rather than differences and exclusion. Transcendent religious people typically are not evangelical. Their outlook is that different religions are suited to different people and that different religions are manifestations of the same essential truths.

Transcendent religious people reject the idea that humans are fundamentally defective in some way in favor of the idea that all of us are basically good—and that we all are doing the best we can under our given circumstances. Whereas the unconscious purpose of egoic religion is to strengthen the ego through dogma, judgments, and group identity, the purpose of transcendent religion is the complete opposite: to transcend the ego through love, compassion, and spiritual practice.

The ego keeps its hold on and is central to egoic religion, whereas those able to break the bounds of ego practice true spiritually based transcendent religion. These two ways of practicing religion are why religion is capable of producing some of the most hateful figures and appalling acts, but also of some of the most noble and compassionate. This is why religion has produced both Osama Bin Laden and Archbishop Desmond Tutu. The acts of savagery carried out in the name of egoic religion dominate the news, but more quietly, transcendent religious people are expressing some of the highest aspects of their authentic spiritual nature.

Transcendent religion sees through the illusion of separation with the knowledge that truth is universal. Several open-minded spiritual teachers and researchers have sought to identify the commonality between the world's great religions, rather than focusing on their differences. As Ralph Waldo Trine wrote in the introductory quote to this chapter, "There is a golden thread that runs through every religion in the world." This golden thread encompasses the common truths identified by enlightened spiritual visionaries throughout history.

As the American philosopher Ernest Holmes writes in his 1948 book *How to Use the Science of Mind*, "We should waste no time in futile arguments as to what religion or spiritual outlook is right or wrong, but gladly accept the evidence of anyone's prayer and faith as a demonstration of that person's belief. Too much time is lost in arguing whether or not one's philosophy is the only correct one, her religion the only true one, his method of procedure the only effective one. Let us leave these arguments to the contentions of smaller minds and try to find the thread of Truth running through all systems. Let us build on the affirmative and forget the negative."

The 19th century Indian Hindu mystic Ramakrishna states: "God has made different religions to suit different aspirations, times, and countries. All doctrines are only so many paths; but a path is by no means God Himself. Indeed, one can reach God if one follows any of the paths with wholehearted devotion." Ramakrishna's enlightened perspective points out that while different religions have different teachers, customs, and practices, every religion can be a vehicle to arrive at the ultimate truth.

What are these universal truths that define the golden thread? Volumes have been written on this topic by Huston Smith, C. David Lundberg, and several others. Here is a summary of these findings:

1. Love Is the Permeating Principle

Realization of love is the ultimate goal of life. Despite outward appearances of negativity and suffering in the world, love permeates all of creation. Only love is real. Joy is the result of living in close harmony with God's love.

"Full of love for all things in the world, practicing virtue in order to benefit others, this man is truly happy."

— Buddhism, *The Dhammapada*

2. Unity of All Things

We are all part of the One God. God is present in all of creation. Separation is an illusion. We are God in action, co-creating with the one divine power.

"He is the one God, hidden in all beings, all-pervading, the self within all beings, watching over all works, dwelling in all beings, the witness, the perceiver, the only one. ... He is the one ruler of many who seem to act, but really do not act; he makes the one seed manifold. The wise who perceive him within their self, to them belongs eternal happiness, not to others."

— Hinduism, *Svetasvatara Upanishad*, VI

3. Have Faith and Hope in God

Faith maintains our connection to God and ability to see the good in all things. Through our faith in God, we direct God's divine energy in our life for right action. Faith and hope allow us to overcome obstacles and suffering to manifest good things in our life and in those we touch.

"Now faith is the substance of things hoped for, the evidence of things not seen. ... Through faith we understand that the worlds were framed by the word of God. ... But without faith it is impossible to please him: for he that cometh to God must believe that He is, and that He is a rewarder of them that diligently seek him."

— Christianity and Judaism, *The Bible*, Hebrews 11:1, 3, 6

4. Love the Divine in Yourself

Since God is everywhere, all knowing and all powerful, He is within us. We are spirit inhabiting a human body. It is good and right to love the divinity within us. It is not the Divine Self that needs forgiveness but the acts we commit as our lower, egoic human selves. It is essential to forgive ourselves and let go of all guilt and shame.

"To be a musician one must send out a melody; and to be master of music requires hours of practice. So to be a master of the divine gift of love one must practice, and he is both the instrument and the musician, for upon his own being is the divine melody played, first with himself, then within the heart of others."

— Confucianism, *Ye are Gods,* Annalee Skarin

5. Love the Divine in Others

In reality we are one large universal family. We love someone when we look for and see God and good in them. Forgiveness of egoic acts from others entails seeing them from the perspective of love. If someone tries to hurt another, it means they are perceiving that person as something separate and foreign from themselves.

"Not one of you is a believer until he loves for his brother what he loves for himself."

— Islam, *Forty Hadith of An-Nawawi,* 13

6. Do Your Work with Love

Applying inner vision to earthly works, as an extension of faith, is a great key to divine power. Right thoughts lead to right action. For love to flow freely, it is important to love what you do. Whatever you do for a living should help others in some way. By serving others, you will experience greater levels of inner peace and fulfillment.

"From this time forward, arm yourself with courage, and banish all impure and unworthy thoughts that may present themselves to your mind. You must first bring forth a crop of pure and noble thoughts, and after that you may direct your efforts to the accomplishment of good. If an opportunity comes to do good action which is within the limits of your strength, hasten to do it with a firm and resolute heart, without calculating whether it is large or small, difficult or easy, or whether it will bring you any advantage."

— Taoism, *T'ai-Shang Kan-Ying P'ien, The Spirit of the Hearth*

7. You Reap What You Sow

We eventually have to face up to the consequences of our actions. We have a choice between acting from ego or acting from spirit. If we do destructive actions, we are going to put into place bad conditions that adversely affect us in the future. Conversely, loving actions result in love returning to us.

"Do not be deceived: God is not mocked, for whatever one sows, that will he also reap. For the one who sows to his own flesh will from the flesh reap corruption, but the one who sows to the Spirit will from the Spirit reap eternal life. And let us not grow weary of doing good, for in due season we will reap, if we do not give up."

— Christianity, *The Bible*, Galatians 6:7-9

8. Eternal Life

Our human bodies decay and die, but our spiritual essence, or soul, lives for eternity. Eternal life functions outside of and beyond time, as well as within time. Religions differ in the belief of reincarnation, but all contend that our spirit continues beyond death in some form.

"For behold, this is my work and my glory—to bring to pass the immortality and eternal life of man."

— Mormonism, *Pearl of Great Price*, Moses 1:39

The commonality in the above religious concepts is transcendence of ego, realization of our higher spiritual nature, and acting from love rather than fear. These pursuits can be seen as the very purpose of religion and our human life. Transcendent religion is a key component of our evolution beyond the chains that our egos place on us. Religion practiced from this perspective results in a blessing to ourselves and those around us, and it contributes to raising the consciousness of the entire planet.

In the next chapter we explore the role of ego and spirit in our most intimate relationships.

CH9

The Nature of Romantic Relationships

Much of what we do as partners is fundamentally about survival and our beastly, instinctual selves.

Stan Tatkin
2011

Slipping the bounds of our egoic nature
and relating to romantic partners from
an enlightened viewpoint is a major
challenge for those on a spiritual path.

From the perspective of evolution, our life's purpose culminates in finding a mate and producing offspring. Therefore, our egoic drives and emotions are at their most extreme when pursuing this goal. Romantic relationships carry such power to induce intense emotions that humankind is constantly thinking, writing, singing, laughing, or crying about them. Their ability to bring us to a state of ecstatic bliss can create an obsession to find that perfect union. The sorrow that can be born from them creates a deep-seated fear of their ability to cause pain in our most vulnerable places. The strong emotions present in the courtship and pair-bonding process are a testament to the high genetic stakes in play.

The intra-psychic dance between love and fear is most apparent in our romantic relationships. When falling in love, our ego's drives for protection and competition are temporarily suspended. Our ego's selfish and defensive propensities are overcome by the romantic drive toward intimacy and vulnerability. As the relationship continues, we strive to maintain the delight of falling in love in the face of the ego's fearful intrusions. Despite our efforts, our egos often retract in fear at the moments we wish to reach out with love.

In this chapter, we explore the biological underpinnings of romantic relationships and some solutions to relationship problems created by the ego. We also investigate the realm of transcendent relationships and potential paths toward that end. Becoming conscious of our ego's influence on how we relate and finding healthy alternatives is an important step in creating functional and fulfilling relationships. Intimate relationships can be a proving ground for sorting out egoic altruism that expects a return on investment versus true transcendent unconditional love. At their best, romantic relationships become a spiritual path that propels lovers beyond ego toward enlightenment.

How Ego and Biology Impact Romantic Relationships

Some part of us is aware that our ego's defensiveness, blame, jealousy, and need to be right can slowly destroy our relationships, yet we feel powerless to stop it. Fears and egoic wounds can lay dormant for years until a romantic relationship stirs the pot and brings them front and center. Intimate relationships present an opportunity to heal these wounds with the support of a loving partner. However, there is also a risk of reinforcing the old wounds if previous patterns are repeated. Therefore, our happiness and fragile self-esteem seem to be inextricably tied to success in romance.

To understand the egoic aspects of romantic relationships, it is necessary to reveal the biological basis for romantic pairing. Biology and evolutionary psychology are the furthest things from the mind of the lover caught up in the extreme emotions induced by romantic relationships. But underneath the obsessive thoughts and intense emotions, decidedly unromantic human biology is hard at work to facilitate the evolutionary goals of pair bonding, reproduction, and child rearing. Through natural selection, nature has provided us with a host of instinctive behaviors and neurochemicals to facilitate these subconscious goals.

Let's take a look at how human pair bonding and reproduction evolved. Taking a step back from the human reproductive process, we can ask: Why do we have two genders to begin with? Why not one or three genders? It turns out there are some species of lizards and insects that have only one gender employing asexual reproduction. Offspring are an exact genetic match of the parent. In some respects, this is a more efficient system because all individuals of the species can reproduce, not just the female half. So once again, why two genders?

The answer again stems from evolutionary biology. Natural selection is driven by genetic variability. Genetic mutations that contribute to evolutionary fitness are preserved, and those that don't are eliminated from the gene pool. This genetic variability is driven in part by mixing the genes of two different individuals to produce offspring with unique gene combinations. Some of these offspring with unique genes may hold the key to increased evolutionary fitness. For more advanced species, mixing of the immune systems of different individuals may increase disease resistance as well. Therefore, the two-gender reproductive system won out in the evolutionary competition.

Fast forwarding a few hundred million years from the first two-gender species, we find humans still employing the two-gender reproductive strategy, but with a high level of complexity and sophistication. Humans produce very few offspring, and these offspring require a long maturation period with a large investment of time and resources from the parents. Women in particular must be extremely dedicated to their children, as they can only produce one child a year who requires a large investment of nutrients from the mother's body. Having both the mother and father present for gestating and raising the child greatly increases the chances of the child surviving to a reproductive age. Ideally, both parents provide resources, nurturing, and protection for the child. Therefore, humans primarily employ monogamous pair bonding as the preferred reproductive strategy. Selection of the best mate to maximize the chance of success in producing and raising healthy, attractive children is a high-stakes dating game for humans.

Pair bonding is crucial to reproduction and child rearing in humans. In the courtship phase of a relationship, neurochemicals such as dopamine and oxytocin are released to create a strong bond between prospective parents. These chemicals create the excitement, bliss, and singular focus on the beloved that is familiar to those that have fallen in love. Release of these chemicals continues for about a year, corresponding to what is commonly referred to as the honeymoon phase. In this phase, one's partner is seen as the source of the blissful feelings and is therefore idealized. Lovers are on their best behavior in this phase. Any character flaws or egoic patterns in the loved one are typically ignored or rationalized away during this honeymoon period, in service to maintaining the pair bond. In our evolutionary history, nature provided this honeymoon phase to maintain the coupling long enough to produce a child.

Once these bonding neurochemicals begin to subside, our egoic tendencies return to the forefront. The blinders come off and we begin to see our lover's ego in operation. Blissful feelings are often replaced by the egoic emotions of fear, jealousy, or anger when the beloved does not meet our expectations. Partners may blame each other for the end of the bliss. Manipulative and controlling behaviors can appear in an attempt to get our partner to conform to our desires. Once past the honeymoon phase, relationships have a way of exposing dysfunctional patterns and maladaptive egoic behaviors in living color. Any egoic wounds, such as an insecure attachment style, begin to drive relationship dynamics. The end of the honeymoon phase often leads to conflict and disillusionment for lovers.

Couples typically face a decision at this point. Now that you know your partner better and see them more clearly, do you jump ship in hopes of finding a better relationship, or do you hang in there and attempt to overcome the problems? Are there intractable problems in the relationship, such as verbal or physical abuse, that are unlikely to change? Are there long-standing mental health or addiction issues? Are both partners willing to take personal responsibility in the relationship, or do partners blame each other for the problems? Partners who have a secure attachment style or have addressed their egoic wounding will likely have an easier time transitioning out of the honeymoon period to a securely functioning long-term relationship.

Moving Beyond Egoic Relationships

If the couple chooses to stay together, the real journey toward a healthy and conscious relationship can begin. Partners recognize that the biological drives and neurochemicals that created the pair bond have dissipated for good, and a new basis for the purpose and meaning of the relationship is needed. Couples pursuing a path of personal and spiritual growth will consciously commit to the relationship as a powerful vehicle for exploration and healing. They prioritize the relationship and protect it from destructive influences. Each takes personal responsibility for their own behavior and the impact it has on the relationship. The relationship then provides an opportunity to move past endless egoic reactions and awaken to our true nature. When we approach relationships in this way, they become a spiritual path—an unfolding process of personal and spiritual development.

Although the two-gender pair bonding system evolved from biological imperatives, conscious couples can use this intimate two-person system for mutual exploration and healing. Areas to explore in the safe setting the relationship can provide include past wounds, emotional vulnerability, unconditional love, unconscious expectations, repressed needs and desires, effective communication, common aspirations, and mutual support/emotional regulation. Once we experience new healthy ways of relating within the relationship, they can be rolled out to our interaction with the world in general.

In Chapter 7, we discussed using our emotional triggers as a signpost pointing to where additional healing is needed. This is particularly true in romantic and family relationships where our egoic complexes are most likely to rear their heads. In a conscious relationship, both partners strive to look under the hood of the egoic reaction to find and address the root cause. Often, the root cause predates the relationship, stemming from dynamics in the family of origin or wounds from previous relationships.

Here are some tips and tools for dealing with relationship issues stemming from egoic patterns.

- **Limbic Hijack**—Communication can quickly break down into an argument when both partners' egos are fully engaged. To change this pattern, begin by noticing when you or your partner move from calm discussion to a heated argument. This is the point where the neocortex—the seat of logical thought—loses control of our reaction and the emotional limbic brain starts driving our behavior. Our instinctive fight-or-flight response is triggered. This point is termed a *limbic hijack* because the emotional limbic brain rather than the logical neocortex starts controlling our behavior. Little constructive communication is likely to occur once we reach this point. Mutual triggering to higher states of agitation will occur as limbic brains take control and egoic complexes battle it out.

The best solution to this problem is to interrupt the escalation pattern by taking a break from interacting. Our brains need some time to calm down and shift control back to the neocortex. Both partners should make an agreement ahead of time that either can call a timeout when communication gets out of hand. The couple should also make an agreement about when they will reconvene to finish the discussion.

- **To Protect or Learn**—Our ego's main purpose is to protect us from external threats. This becomes a problem when the external threat is perceived to come from our partner. When operating from ego with our partner, fear, anger, defensiveness, the need to control, and the need to be right are engaged to protect our self-esteem. Listening to and understanding our partner does not occur when these ego mechanisms are in operation. Self-reflection and awareness of our part in the conflict is nearly impossible when these defenses are engaged.

No real progress is made in resolving a conflict until fear subsides and we begin to be curious about what's behind the conflict. A shift in consciousness is needed to move from the intent to protect our ego to an intent to learn about our partner and ourselves. This shift from protection to learning requires us to transition from seeing our partner as an adversary to seeing them as our fellow explorer. Couples must learn to be present with uncomfortable emotions without lashing out to accomplish this. As stated above, often a break in the conversation is needed to make this shift.

The intent to learn entails a willingness to be vulnerable in discussing our part of the conflict and a willingness to be kind and open-hearted toward our partner. Compassion emerges from acceptance that both partners are human, with built-in egos that are naturally fearful. Judgments and defensiveness are replaced by curiosity and acceptance. Embracing compassion encourages our partner to be vulnerable as well, which leads to true mutual understanding. Expressing compassion toward our partner as they reveal painful memories or feelings of shame about themselves creates a powerful healing experience. Such experiences build intimacy and strengthen the bond between partners. A resolution to the conflict with both partners getting their needs met flows naturally when we stay open hearted with an intent to learn.

- **The Do-Over**—Our ego's defenses instinctually engage when we perceive a threat. Our protective response is often automatic, occurring before we are aware of what's happening. Old dysfunctional patterns of communication, born from ego and poor childhood role models, are typically our first response when threatened. Conflicts can spiral out of control quickly, and hurtful words are said with lightning speed.

The damage done to the relationship needs to be repaired, and one of the best ways of accomplishing this is with the "do-over." The do-over is an agreement to go back to the original trigger that started an argument and discuss the topic with a calmer and more thoughtful approach. The do-over should be done once the limbic hijack has subsided and both partners are able to shift from the intent to protect to the intent to learn.

Partners agree to let go of the painful words expressed and focus on healthy communication and mutual kindness. Sharing emotions and needs from an attitude of personal responsibility is key to a successful do-over. Using only "I" statements (I think…, I feel…, I want…) is a good start in taking personal responsibility. Partners immediately feel defensive when critical "you" statements are expressed (you are…, you should have… you don't…), so "you" statements should be avoided at all costs. A successful do-over overwrites the damaging argument in our brains and brings us back into synchronization with our partner.

- **Attachment Style**—In Chapter 3, we introduced the idea of attachment style—the style of relating we learned with primary caregivers in childhood. This attachment style is carried forward to adulthood and determines how we are likely to relate to romantic partners. There are two general types: *secure attachment* and *insecure attachment.* Secure attachments occur when a child's needs for physical and emotional nurturing are consistently met by parents/caregivers. The child learns to trust that the caregiver will be there for them when needed, and this trust is generalized to other people as the child grows.

Insecure attachments occur when caregivers are either inconsistently available to the child or mostly absent in meeting the child's needs. Inconsistent availability results in an *insecure-anxious attachment* style, where the child often wonders when the caregiver will be available and when they will not. This inconsistency induces fear and anxiety in the child, as they cannot depend on the caregiver to be available. This uncertainty about trustworthiness is transferred to others as they become adults, and their anxiety becomes part of the egoic complex. They will be susceptible to feelings of abandonment as an adult.

An insecure-avoidant attachment style occurs when the caregiver is generally not available to meet the child's needs. Any interaction with the caregiver is usually of a critical nature. The child unconsciously decides their needs will never be met and gives up on the caregiver. They attempt to be self-sufficient and try not to depend on anyone. People with an insecure-avoidant attachment style often grow up to be depression-prone loners and have a difficult time trusting anyone. Even a caring and trustworthy partner may be met with suspicion and distrust.

Our attachment style is woven together with our ego's genetic propensities and the impact of other childhood experiences, such as any abuse or trauma, to create our particular egoic complex. Our attachment style and egoic complex have an immense impact on the quality and functioning of adult relationships. Conscious couples will seek to understand their own and their partners' egoic complex and meet both with curiosity, kindness, and understanding.

- **Interlocking Egoic Complexes**—As if dealing with our individual egoic complexes were not enough, partners' complexes can interact to trigger reciprocal egoic reactions that quickly escalate into an explosion of emotions. For example, consider Lisa with an insecure-anxious attachment style whose partner, Mark, has an insecure-avoidant attachment style. Lisa experienced repeated feelings of rejection in childhood and is therefore hyper aware of any signs that Mark is withdrawing from her. Her confirmation bias causes her to constantly scan Mark for any indication that he is not 100 percent dedicated to her.

  Mark is most comfortable when alone, so he begins to feel overwhelmed by Lisa's anxious focus on him. His go-to strategy under stress is to withdraw into his own world. His withdrawal escalates Lisa's anxiety and sense of abandonment, which escalates Mark's overwhelm and pushes him further away. As this manner of interaction is repeated, it becomes an entrenched dysfunctional pattern of relating that can destroy the relationship.

A multitude of combinations of egoic complexes are possible, creating the unique relationship dynamics of each couple. Becoming aware of the interlocking pattern and finding ways of relating that are not mutually triggering is critical to the success of a relationship. Partners should strive to develop a deep understanding of their own and each other's history and emotional triggers. Avoiding triggering our partner to the extent possible and contributing to their healing through corrective experiences are key practices for couples on the path to a healthy relationship.

There is some evidence that we unconsciously seek out partners with whom we have interlocking egoic wounding. Our earliest and deepest emotional wounds are inflicted by our parents. We unconsciously seek out partners with similar traits as our parents, particularly the opposite sex parent. This characteristic of coupling stems from our unconscious draw toward familiar people and situations. Such a pairing results in reenactments of family-of-origin drama and in emergence of interlocking egoic wounding. From a spiritual perspective, we may be drawn toward revisiting painful childhood experiences to change the story and heal the wound. Conscious couples become aware of this dynamic and direct their efforts toward changing the destructive pattern and to mutual healing. Doing so changes a potentially rewounding experience to a healing experience.

Egoic wounds and insecure attachments primarily developed in relationship to childhood caregivers, and healing of these wounds requires healthy adult relationships. Healthy romantic relationships can be ideal vehicles to accomplish this healing. However, sometimes effective relating to a psychotherapist or loving friend is needed before we are capable of staying grounded in the face of the intense emotions romantic relationships bring. Conscious individuals may choose to seek out healing platonic relationships prior to entering romantic relationships. Personal growth entails both individual practices and experience in healthy relating with another.

The above tools and practices primarily address ego-based wounds and dysfunctional behaviors in an attempt to move past the negative consequences they have on relationships. There is another realm of exploration for the couple on the path toward enlightenment. This is the realm of relationships as a spiritual path.

Relationships as a Spiritual Path

When we view our time on Earth as an opportunity to mature spiritually, intimate relationships become one of the most important avenues to that end. For intimate relationships to become a spiritual path, some traditional views of relationship must be held under the light of scrutiny. We must reframe the purpose of relationship from the idea that they are to make us happy to the concept of relationship as a vehicle for healing and growth. With this view, problems and conflict in relationships are seen as opportunities for growth and a chance to clear whatever is unlike love within us. Armed with this attitude, along with an intent to dedicate the time and energy necessary to move from fear to love, love relationships become an exciting journey of discovery and healing.

The challenges of forging an authentic connection with another person inevitably spur us to become more conscious, to examine ourselves more deeply, and to develop greater intention, courage, and awareness in the way we live. Relationships have enormous power as vehicles for mutual healing—physical, emotional, and spiritual. Intimate relationships are a path toward opening the heart so that the wounds of the past and the confusion of the present are received in mercy and awareness. Those in a conscious, committed relationship work mindfully with all that arises in the heart and mind. Using all that arises to work on oneself, as grist for the mill of deep inner growth, allows the unconscious to become conscious. Our spiritual commitment to truth and integrity creates a safe harbor within us—a mooring to return to when the journey gets rough. Love can resurrect our most primitive feelings of fear, hope, dependency, and abandonment. If we know how to stay connected to spirit, soothe our pain, and relax into our emptiness in the midst of these intense feelings, we are well on the way to spiritual partnership. As we move deeper into presence and embrace our spiritual essence, relationship issues become ripples on the surface of the water rather than torrid storms.

Transcendence in Union

In Chapter 7 we discussed entering transcendent states of presence as an individual. It's also possible to transcend ego in conjunction with a partner. In such experiences, the primary focus is on transcending the illusion of separation between partners. When in a transcendent state of love with another, ego boundaries dissolve and we become more fully present and connected with ourselves and our partners. This state of oneness with our beloved is intimate, expansive, and enlivening. In these moments of heightened presence, we no longer need to defend or prove ourselves. Something in us relaxes. Our usual cares and distractions fade into the background, and we feel more awake and aware. We experience what it is like just to be present with another and to be fully accepted as ourselves. Common disagreements seem silly and petty in such a state, and only love is real.

Such experiences of union can happen spontaneously whenever couples are in a state of presence and turn their attention toward each other. Mutual transcendent states can also be cultivated. Here are a few practices for couples who wish to pursue transcendent states together.

- **Eye Gazing**—Shakespeare wrote, "The eyes are the window to the soul." Eye gazing is an ancient practice found in Buddhist and Hindu tantra, as well as in Sufism. Modern psychology confirms that eye gazing is one of the fastest ways to build intimacy. When we gaze deeply into our beloved's eyes, we feel more connected to their soul, as they are to ours. We can see beyond their physical body and ego into their essence. When both partners stay in presence, ego boundaries dissolve and we experience a state of ecstatic union.

    Eye gazing can also bring any blocks to intimacy into awareness. Fears and judgments may arise as we peer into our lover's eyes. We may feel uncomfortably vulnerable. Be aware of any thoughts and emotions that emerge while eye gazing. After eye gazing, discuss these with your partner in a kind and curious manner. This is an excellent opportunity to clear these blocks to intimacy.

- **Sensuality and Sexuality**—Intense sensory experiences pull our attention into the present moment and clear the mind. Sensuality and sexuality are excellent vehicles for couples to reach a state of presence together. Ego boundaries dissolve and a relaxed vulnerability emerges when we surrender to our lover's touch. When making love, our awareness of senses and emotions heightens, and we experience the moment from a place of openness. An active merging of body and spirit takes place. Problems and conflicts fade away and everything is perfect, if only for a few minutes.

    Such moments can serve as an anchor and reference point to return to when ego tightens its grip once again. Once we know that the ego's illusions can be vanquished, it becomes easier to return to a state of presence beyond ego, either with our partner or alone.

- **Co-creative Process**—Many of us have experienced a state of flow when deeply emerged in a creative project or engaging work. Our logical thought, intuition, and emotions seem to flow together in a synergistic manner to create something that was not previously in our awareness. This process of manifestation is gratifying because the past and future dissolve and we are immersed in the present moment. A sense of pride and satisfaction follows the creative experience.

    Less common is to enter this state of flow with another person. The co-creative process requires us to enter this state of flow together. The ego's desire to be right, to be superior, to take credit must be dissolved in favor of a seamless melding of insights and ideas. In this state, two minds become one, such that thoughts, intuitions, and images seem to originate from a common mind. The creation cannot be traced back to an individual partner. A high level of trust and relaxation into union is needed to achieve egoless co-creation. Doing so results in enhanced intimacy and relationship satisfaction.

    A simple way to practice co-creation is to make up a story together. One partner starts the story with one sentence, then the other contributes the next sentence. Partners take turns adding sentences until the story comes to an end. A state of flow is reached when there is a sense of delight in the process with no resistance to our partner's contributions. Any judgments or frustrations that arise can be explored together with curiosity.

Relationships inevitably bring us up against our most painful unresolved egoic wounds from the past—all our worst fears, neuroses, and dysfunctional patterns—in full bloom. When we unconsciously follow the ego's directives, we fall further into the abyss of painful emotions that relationships can bring. Becoming aware of how ego can negatively impact our relationships and working to move beyond the ego's grip creates loving, secure relationships. The willingness to wholeheartedly embrace both the joy and painful realizations that relationships bring propels us along the path to enlightened relationships.

The relationship skills and spiritual maturity we attain in the intimate two-person system of romantic relationships can be a springboard for bringing love and healing to the world. In the next and final chapter, we discuss bringing our enlightened perspective to the world in general.

CH10

Your Enlightened Ego in the World

The spiritual life does not remove us from the world but leads us deeper into it.

Henri J.M. Nouwen
1981

As Seth grew into a young man
and started a family with his beloved,
he continued to feel the pull of spirit
as he went about the daily tasks
of survival.

He was particularly drawn to the tribal shaman and spent any spare time at his feet, soaking in his wisdom. He learned that hunting was a deeply spiritual activity and the killing of an animal was not its death in the conventional sense of the word but as the release of its soul. The dances and other rituals performed were a moral obligation to the animal and its powerful guardian spirit. He learned how to construct tumuli, or burial mounds, and the rituals required to assist the passing of deceased tribal members into the spirit world. His connection to nature became a means to realize the interconnection of all beings. Most importantly, Seth learned to tune into the world of the unseen and commune with spirit.

As both Seth's father, the tribal chief, and the tribal shaman approach their passing, Seth is faced with a choice. He has the opportunity to take his father's position as chief, with the power and resources that come with the position, or he can become the tribal shaman and focus his life on the world of spirit. Seth's sense of inner knowing and unity of all living beings is quite strong. In his heart, the choice is clear. Seth still feels the pull of his ego toward power and dominance, but the pull toward the spiritual world is stronger. Seth decides to take over the role of shaman and spends his remaining years providing spiritual guidance to the tribe. His focus shifts from his own survival to the well-being of others. He never again picks up a weapon.

Seth and his contemporaries did not have access to spiritual teachings in the modern sense. In today's world, we have a wide variety of religious and spiritual teachings, as well as myriad egoic distractions. Modern life often feels overwhelming. In a sense, Seth had an advantage over us. He led a simple life, close to the earth and the beings that inhabit it. He naturally developed the ability to be present with himself and his environment. He learned to tune into his inner knowing rather than being told what to believe. His spirituality grew from within rather than being forced from without. As his spirituality matured, he naturally transitioned from preoccupation with himself to a caring awareness of other tribal members and the natural world.

Fostering Compassion

As our spirituality matures, the focus on ourselves subsides and we become more concerned with the well-being of all sentient beings. As our compassion grows, we recognize the suffering around us and take action to help. Compassion embodies a tangible expression of love for those around us. True compassion is not a quick pat on the head, but instead requires a deep understanding and acceptance of the truth about ourselves and others. Compassion acts on this knowledge by loving the truth we find.

The grand illusion of ego is that we are separate beings who must be defensive and competitive with one another. Ego believes others are out to get us so we must stay on high alert: "You have to look out for number one." This attitude makes it nearly impossible to be compassionate with others, or ourselves for that matter. One of the ego's secrets is that we are critical of others to the same degree we are critical of ourselves. As within, so without. This truth is an avenue to finding compassion for those critical of us–realizing they are critical of themselves to the same extent. Our interconnectedness makes it impossible to be kind to ourselves while being critical of others, because others are just a reflection of us.

We are accustomed to labeling those around us as good or bad, right or wrong, acceptable or unacceptable. This is our ego's shorthand method of identifying who is a threat and who is not. The problem is that at our core, we are inseparable from others, so we make the same judgments of ourselves. Therefore, true compassion must be universal. We cannot be judgmental of others and maintain compassion for ourselves. Conversely, we cannot maintain compassion for others while being judgmental of ourselves. Trying to do so is to remain under the spell of the ego.

Most of us struggle to develop compassion, particularly toward those we judge to be dangerous or inferior. When compassion is difficult, we are still struggling with the illusions of ego. We are mentally straining to find love in our hearts when we are still dominated by fear. Sustained compassion for ourselves and others requires a major paradigm shift. This shift is away from the dualities of right or wrong, good or bad. When examined closely, we find these concepts to be an illusion. When we judge others to be good it simply means we feel pleasurable emotions in response to their actions. When we judge others to be bad it means we feel painful emotions in response to their actions. There is no inherent quality of good or bad within any person or situation. Our minds create good and bad through our judgments.

These judgments are born from the ego's desire to seek pleasure, to avoid pain, and to minimize our brain's effort in evaluating the risk in our environment. A quickly applied label of "bad" informs our actions in avoiding a situation perceived to be dangerous. This is an egoic defense engaged in response to our subjective experience. One person may judge an occurrence as good and another person judge it as bad, depending on whether they feel pain or pleasure about the outcome. A simple example is a sporting event where fans of the winning team judge the outcome as good, and fans of the losing team judge it as bad. These labels are born from their perspective on the outcome and the resulting internal emotional state.

The problem is not that we use the terms good and bad. The problem is that we are unaware that this labeling is a subjective ego function, and we actually believe that the qualities of good or bad reside within the person or situation we are labeling. We are unaware that we are generating the ideas of good or bad within ourselves. The Sufi poet Rumi understood this when he wrote, "Out beyond ideas of wrongdoing and rightdoing there is a field. I'll meet you there. When the soul lies down in that grass the world is too full to talk about."

We mistakenly apply the good/bad labels to ourselves just as we apply it to others. This constant self-evaluation against some imaginary standard creates stress and keeps us from living from our authentic self. In addition, when the collective ego of our community judges someone to be bad, it reinforces the attachment to our judgments because we have confirmation from others. If everyone thinks someone is bad, it must be true. Or at least that is what our ego would have us believe.

To seek the truth about ourselves and others takes a more thoughtful and nonjudgmental approach. In reality, everyone is doing the best they can, given their background and circumstances. We are neither good nor bad. From an individual's perspective, everything they do is in their best interest. They think their actions will benefit them in some way. People do not cause pain and suffering because they are bad. They cause pain and suffering because they are acting from a distorted view of reality. They believe they are separate and unaffected by their actions toward others and that they can gain from another's loss.

The more distorted a person's perspective on reality, the more likely their actions will cause pain to those around them and to themselves. Forensic psychologists study the motivations and mental characteristics of criminals from this viewpoint. When the psyche of a violent criminal is investigated, invariably they find an abusive childhood and difficult life circumstances, sometimes coupled with a genetic propensity toward mental illness. Criminals are not inherently bad or evil. To them, there are valid reasons why they behave the way they do.

The same goes for all of humanity—none of us are inherently bad or evil. Such judgments are based on an illusion. Holding this new perspective opens the door for sustained compassion that is not subject to our moment-to-moment egoic reactions. Love and acceptance of others becomes a natural part of the flow of life.

This is not to say we do not set boundaries in response to those causing pain and destruction. Often dangerous people need to be restrained from hurting others. We may exclude people who cause pain and suffering from our lives. However, our protective actions need not be accompanied by anger and judgment. We can have compassion for the suffering of the offender while controlling their behavior or our exposure to them. Labeling them as bad cuts off the compassion within us that might bring them healing.

Shifting our paradigm away from the need to judge others as bad frees us to do the same for ourselves. If no one can be bad or defective, we cannot be either. We are off the hook. The whole egoic illusion evaporates. From this enlightened perspective, compassion flows easily. We see others as we might see a child, as an innocent being doing the best they can. In reality, we are all children on the spiritual path at various stages of development.

To foster compassion rather than criticism, we can return to the approach discussed in Chapter 9 —the intent to learn rather than the intent to protect. Letting go of the need for others to be wrong, we can become curious of what's behind their words and actions. What are they afraid of? How do they think their actions will benefit them? What egoic wounds and triggers are they grappling with? What unexpressed needs do they have? What am I willing to do to meet those needs? Our intent to learn requires us to dispense with easy derogatory labels and spend time investigating with open hearts and minds. It is just as important to extend this kindness and curiosity toward ourselves as it is to others.

Choosing Our Community

When we carry our egoic complex into adulthood, we are often subconsciously attracted to people and situations that feel familiar and confirm our beliefs about the world. This tendency creates a self-fulfilling prophecy, leading to a distorted view of reality that can last a lifetime. To break out of our distorted little world, it's helpful to consciously seek out people who counteract our embedded beliefs. Spending time with such people becomes a healing experience that can overwrite the old negative expectations and rewire the brain to expect love and kindness.

Did you grow up in a physically or verbally abusive environment? Find friends or groups that emphasize the honoring of personal boundaries and nonviolent, compassionate communication. Did you grow up in an addiction-riddled family? Find those who confront problems and emotions directly and are drawn to healthy activities, such as spending time in nature. Were you neglected as a child? Find others who consistently think about your needs and make you a priority in their life. We may find we have actually been avoiding such beneficial people because they feel unfamiliar and confusing. They do not match up with our expectations. It may take time to feel comfortable around such people. Given time, healthy relationships will begin to feel normal.

Once we are able to release the illusions of ego, many of our neurotic thoughts and habits toward others melt away. The ego's constant worry about what people think of us disappears. The fear of rejection when being vulnerable with others relaxes. The mental energy we expend judging ourselves and others becomes available to use in more enlightened pursuits. The striving for excessive money, power, and status is no longer necessary, and we have more time and energy available for the benefit of our community. We see that there is no difference between actions benefiting ourselves or others because we see our neighbor as ourself.

Reaching out to friends, family, and community from this enlightened perspective is a joyful process of spreading love to all who cross our path. It also serves as a magnet to draw others to us who have a similar orientation. A loving community grows, one authentic connection at a time. The power of love multiplies, creating a strong and resilient web that becomes a force for positive change in the world.

Enlightened Work

As people become busier and our lives ever more work-centric, it is more important than ever to carry our spirituality into the workplace. When we begin to embody oneness with all beings in our daily life, our focus naturally evolves from solely our own well-being to the well-being of all of humanity. We are drawn to compassionate acts for the benefit of all living beings. Enlightenment is both a state of being and right action in our world.

We can endeavor to use our personal power well in order to love, connect, heal, protect, and make our gifts and our purpose manifest in the world. We derive satisfaction from physically, emotionally, and spiritually supporting others, regardless of any reciprocal benefit. Such right action need not be grandiose or require a career change to become a spiritual guru. We can apply spiritual principles to any job by being aware, effective, and compassionate toward colleagues and customers.

When our ego is engaged at work, separation and competition become our reality. We find ourselves competing with colleagues for admiration and superior positions. Money is the carrot for which everyone strives. We may be deceptive or manipulative in pursuing this singular goal. Our ancient genetic drive to acquire power and resources is engaged to the detriment of other life priorities. As other areas of life suffer from neglect, workaholism or other addictions may result in an attempt to suppress our sadness and disappointment with life. Blindly following egoic drives in work leads to unending striving, disappointment, and frustration.

Being mindful of these egoic drives and the transcendent alternatives is one of the most valuable things we can do to bring our spirituality to work each day. Make a conscious effort to bring your enlightened perspective to your thoughts and actions. Be aware of your behavior in your work environment and how it affects those around you. Think about what you are saying and the words you are using before you speak them. Notice how other people react to them. Notice how others in the office treat one another and think of ways you can improve this. Look for opportunities to praise and support others in their work. If you are fully aware of your actions and words, you will make decisions that align with your values.

If searching for a new position, investigate working for companies that strive to make the world a better place. Pay attention to the company's mission and values. Who are they helping, and how are they treating people both inside and outside the company? Does the culture include a healthy work/life balance? Do they consider the social and environmental impacts as well as the financial results of their actions? If you want to make a career change, choose a career that is in alignment with your core beliefs and natural gifts. Focus your efforts on work that gives back to the world and makes it a better place.

Closing

As Seth has taught us, true spirituality is not complex. Just stop and be present in this moment. Notice your body and your spiritual essence. Relax into unity with all of life. That's it! Our ego wants to make something that is quite simple into a complicated and unattainable goal. This is a smoke-screen, obscuring the truth from us.

Personal and spiritual growth is more a case of uncovering what is already within us rather than adding more to us. Our work then is to release anything that keeps us from abiding in this sacred simplicity. Rather than learning, we must unlearn. We must unlearn what a critical parent told us about ourselves and embrace ourselves as whole and complete spiritual beings. We must unlearn what our culture taught us about how to achieve happiness. We must release the façade we created in order to be acceptable to others. We must let go of needing to perform to be seen as worthy. We must see through the illusions of ego and live from our eternal spiritual self. Our only opportunity is now.

Appendix

Guided Meditations

GUIDED MEDITATIONS TO AID A SHIFT IN CONSCIOUSNESS ON THE TOPICS IN THIS BOOK ARE PROVIDED TO READERS AT www.theenlightenedego.com/meditations.

TOPIC AREAS INCLUDE:

- EGO AWARENESS
- EGO GRATITUDE
- RELEASING FEAR
- EMOTION AS THE OBJECT OF FOCUS
- DEALING WITH NEGATIVE THOUGHTS
- RELEASING MENTAL ADDICTIONS
- NEGATIVITY BIAS AWARENESS
- FOSTERING SELF-COMPASSION
- AFFIRMATIONS OF GRATITUDE
- NOTING JUDGMENTS
- LOVING KINDNESS
- REDUCE ENVY AND CELEBRATE OTHERS
- LIFE AND DEATH
- HIGHER-SELF AWARENESS
- DISSOLVE INTO PRESENCE
- SURRENDER TO SPIRITUAL GUIDANCE

About the Author

KELLY BENINGA

With a broad range of education and experience spanning the fields of science, psychology, and spirituality, Kelly Beninga brings his unique perspective to integrate viewpoints often at odds in contemporary literature.

Beninga holds a bachelor's degree in engineering from Colorado State University and a master's degree in transpersonal psychology from Naropa University. He is a graduate of the Hakomi Institute for mindful, somatic psychotherapy and is a certified Hakomi therapist. He has studied under well-known figures such as John Welwood, Adyashanti, and Stan Tatkin, as well as several Buddhist teachers such as Sakyong Mipham, Bruce Tift, and Orgyen Chowang. Beninga is also a long-time student of evolutionary psychology and has done coursework in the field at MIT.

Beninga spent much of his career in the field of science and high technology, holds several patents, and was most recently the president and CEO of SkyFuel, Inc., a company engaged in research and development and manufacturing of solar power technologies.

He is currently a psychotherapist in private practice in Lakewood, Colorado, and is the founder of The Relationship Works LLC, providing individual and couples counseling, as well as spiritual coaching based on the concepts in *The Enlightened Ego*. Beninga has written many technical documents as well as articles integrating the viewpoints of science, psychology, and spirituality on topics such as climate change, human attachment theory, and divorce recovery. *The Enlightened Ego* is Beninga's first full-length book.

You can reach Kelly Beninga at: www.theenlightenedego.com, kelly@theenlightened.com, or +1 303-903-5523.

Made in the USA
Monee, IL
16 September 2021